Word 2013:
Intermediate

Student Manual

3-Day MOS Series

Word 2013: Intermediate

Chief Executive Officer, Axzo Press:	Ken Wasnock
Series Designer and COO:	Adam A. Wilcox
Vice President, Operations:	Josh Pincus
Director of Publishing Systems Development:	Dan Quackenbush
Writer:	Christopher G. Hale
Keytester:	Cliff Coryea

Trademarks

ILT Series is a trademark of Axzo Press.

Some of the product names and company names used in this book have been used for identification purposes only and may be trademarks or registered trademarks of their respective manufacturers and sellers.

Disclaimer

We reserve the right to revise this publication and make changes from time to time in its content without notice.

ISBN 10: 1-4260-3733-3
ISBN 13: 978-1-4260-3733-7

Printed in the United States of America

1 2 3 4 5 GL 06 05 04 03

Contents

Introduction

After reading this introduction, you will know how to:

A Use ILT Series manuals in general.

B Use prerequisites, a target student description, course objectives, and a skills inventory to properly set your expectations for the course.

C Re-key this course after class.

Topic A: About the manual

ILT Series philosophy

Our manuals facilitate your learning by providing structured interaction with the software itself. While we provide text to explain difficult concepts, the hands-on activities are the focus of our courses. By paying close attention as your instructor leads you through these activities, you will learn the skills and concepts effectively.

We believe strongly in the instructor-led class. During class, focus on your instructor. Our manuals are designed and written to facilitate your interaction with your instructor, and not to call attention to manuals themselves.

We believe in the basic approach of setting expectations, delivering instruction, and providing summary and review afterwards. For this reason, lessons begin with objectives and end with summaries. We also provide overall course objectives and a course summary to provide both an introduction to and closure on the entire course.

Manual components

The manuals contain these major components:

- Table of contents
- Introduction
- Units
- Course summary
- Glossary
- Index

Each element is described below.

Table of contents

The table of contents acts as a learning roadmap.

Introduction

The introduction contains information about our training philosophy and our manual components, features, and conventions. It contains target student, prerequisite, objective, and setup information for the specific course.

Units

Units are the largest structural component of the course content. A unit begins with a title page that lists objectives for each major subdivision, or topic, within the unit. Within each topic, conceptual and explanatory information alternates with hands-on activities. Units conclude with a summary comprising one paragraph for each topic, and an independent practice activity that gives you an opportunity to practice the skills you've learned.

The conceptual information takes the form of text paragraphs, exhibits, lists, and tables. The activities are structured in two columns, one telling you what to do, the other providing explanations, descriptions, and graphics.

Course summary

This section provides a text summary of the entire course. It is useful for providing closure at the end of the course. The course summary also indicates the next course in this series, if there is one, and lists additional resources you might find useful as you continue to learn about the software.

Glossary

The glossary provides definitions for all of the key terms used in this course.

Index

The index at the end of this manual makes it easy for you to find information about a particular software component, feature, or concept.

Manual conventions

We've tried to keep the number of elements and the types of formatting to a minimum in the manuals. This aids in clarity and makes the manuals more classically elegant looking. But there are some conventions and icons you should know about.

Item	Description
Italic text	In conceptual text, indicates a new term or feature.
Bold text	In unit summaries, indicates a key term or concept. In an independent practice activity, indicates an explicit item that you select, choose, or type.
`Code font`	Indicates code or syntax.

`Longer strings of ▶`
`code will look ▶`
`like this.`
	In the hands-on activities, any code that's too long to fit on a single line is divided into segments by one or more continuation characters (▶). This code should be entered as a continuous string of text.

Select **bold item**	In the left column of hands-on activities, bold sans-serif text indicates an explicit item that you select, choose, or type.
Keycaps like (↵ ENTER)	Indicate a key on the keyboard you must press.

Hands-on activities

The hands-on activities are the most important parts of our manuals. They are divided into two primary columns. The "Here's how" column gives short instructions to you about what to do. The "Here's why" column provides explanations, graphics, and clarifications. Here's a sample:

Do it!

A-1:   Creating a commission formula

Here's how	Here's why
1 Open Sales	This is an oversimplified sales compensation worksheet. It shows sales totals, commissions, and incentives for five sales reps.
2 Observe the contents of cell F4	F4 ▼ = =E4*C_Rate The commission rate formulas use the name "C_Rate" instead of a value for the commission rate.

For these activities, we have provided a collection of data files designed to help you learn each skill in a real-world business context. As you work through the activities, you will modify and update these files. Of course, you might make a mistake and therefore want to re-key the activity starting from scratch. To make it easy to start over, you will rename each data file at the end of the first activity in which the file is modified. Our convention for renaming files is to add the word "My" to the beginning of the file name. In the above activity, for example, a file called "Sales" is being used for the first time. At the end of this activity, you would save the file as "My sales," thus leaving the "Sales" file unchanged. If you make a mistake, you can start over using the original "Sales" file.

In some activities, however, it might not be practical to rename the data file. If you want to retry one of these activities, ask your instructor for a fresh copy of the original data file.

Topic B: Setting your expectations

Properly setting your expectations is essential to your success. This topic will help you do that by providing:

- Prerequisites for this course
- A description of the target student
- A list of the objectives for the course
- A skills assessment for the course

Course prerequisites

Before taking this course, you should be familiar with personal computers and the use of a keyboard and a mouse. Furthermore, this course assumes that you've completed the following course or have equivalent experience:

- *Word 2013:Basic, 3-Day MOS Series*

Target student

The target student for this course is an individual who wants to work more efficiently in Word 2013. You will use styles and outlines, format table, create SmartArt diagrams, draw shapes, format text graphically, create sections and format text in columns, use themes and design elements, manage document revisions, and perform a mail merge.

Course objectives

These overall course objectives will give you an idea about what to expect from the course. It is also possible that they will help you see that this course is not the right one for you. If you think you either lack the prerequisite knowledge or already know most of the subject matter to be covered, you should let your instructor know that you think you are misplaced in the class.

After completing this course, you will know how to:

- Examine and compare text formatting, work with character styles, and work with a document outline.
- Apply table formatting and styles, and work with data in a table.
- Use SmartArt to create and modify a diagram, insert and modify shapes, format text using WordArt, create drop caps, and insert text boxes.
- Insert section breaks, format section headers and footers and page numbering, format text into multiple columns, and customize a document's appearance by applying background colors, fill effects, watermarks, and themes.
- Protect a document with a password, view and edit document properties, use Track Changes, work with comments, and use the Compatibility Checker, the Accessibility Checker, and the Document Inspector to share documents.
- Use the Mailings tab to create form letters, create a recipient list, sort and filter records, and create mailing-label and envelope documents.

Skills inventory

Use the following form to gauge your skill level entering the class. For each skill listed, rate your familiarity from 1 to 5, with five being the most familiar. *This is not a test.* Rather, it is intended to provide you with an idea of where you're starting from at the beginning of class. If you're wholly unfamiliar with all the skills, you might not be ready for the class. If you think you already understand all of the skills, you might need to move on to the next course in the series. In either case, you should let your instructor know as soon as possible.

Skill	1	2	3	4	5
Creating, applying, and modifying styles					
Creating an outline					
Applying borders and shading to tables					
Working with table styles					
Working with data in a table					
Working with fields					
Working with SmartArt					
Drawing and modifying shapes					
Using WordArt					
Inserting drop caps and text boxes					
Creating sections in documents					
Formatting text into columns					
Adding background colors, fill effects, and borders					
Adding a watermark					
Applying themes					
Using Track Changes					
Working with comments					
Comparing and combining documents					
Finalizing documents					
Performing a mail merge					
Preparing mailing labels and envelopes					

Topic C: Re-keying the course

If you have the proper hardware and software, you can re-key this course after class. This section explains what you'll need in order to do so, and how to do it.

Hardware requirements

Your personal computer should have:

- A keyboard and a mouse
- 1 GHz or faster x86- or x64-bit processor with SSE2 instruction set
- 1GB RAM (or higher)
- 3 GB of available hard drive space after the operating system is installed
- A monitor with at least 1024 × 768 resolution

Software requirements

You will also need the following software:

- Windows 7 (You can also use Windows 8, but the screen shots in this course were taken using Windows 7, so your screens might look somewhat different.)
- Microsoft Office 2013

Network requirements

The following network components and connectivity are also required for re-keying this course:

- Internet access, for the following purposes:
  - Downloading the latest critical updates and service packs
  - Downloading the Student Data files (if necessary)

Setup instructions to re-key the course

Before you re-key the course, you will need to perform the following steps.

1   Use Windows Update to install all available critical updates and Service Packs.

2   With flat-panel displays, we recommend using the panel's native resolution for best results. Color depth/quality should be set to High (24 bit) or higher.

    Please note that your display settings or resolution may differ from the author's, so your screens might not exactly match the screen shots in this manual.

3   If necessary, reset any Word 2013 defaults that you have changed. If you do not wish to reset the defaults, you can still re-key the course, but some activities might not work exactly as documented.

    a   Reset Track Changes settings to the defaults:

       i   On the Review tab, from the Display for Review list, select Simple Markup.

       ii   Click Show Markup and choose Balloons, Show Only Comments and Formatting in Balloons.

4   If you have the data disc that came with this manual, locate the Student Data folder on it and copy it to the desktop of your computer.

    If you don't have the data disc, you can download the Student Data files for the course:

    a   Connect to www.axzopress.com.

    b   Under Downloads, click Instructor-Led Training.

    c   Browse the subject categories to locate your course. Then click the course title to display a list of available downloads. (You can also access these downloads through our Catalog listings.)

    d   Click the link(s) for downloading the Student Data files.

    e   Create a folder named Student Data on the desktop of your computer.

    f   Double-click the downloaded zip file(s) and drag the contents into the Student Data folder.

Unit 1

Styles and outlines

Complete this unit, and you'll know how to:

A Examine and compare text formatting by using the Reveal Formatting task pane.

B Apply, create, and modify paragraph and character styles.

C Create, organize, and format a document outline.

Topic A: Examining formatting

Explanation

You can tell what formatting you've applied to text by examining the Font and Paragraph dialog boxes or the Home tab. But a faster way to see the details of all of the formatting applied to a selection is to use the Reveal Formatting task pane. In addition, you can use the Reveal Formatting task pane to compare the formatting of two selections.

The Reveal Formatting task pane

The Reveal Formatting task pane displays the font and paragraph formatting of the selected text, as shown in Exhibit 1-1. To open the Reveal Formatting task pane, press Shift+F1. The applied formatting is displayed under "Formatting of selected text." Exhibit 1-1 shows that the heading is formatted as Trebuchet MS, 24 pt, Bold, and has a custom color applied to it. Click the blue underlined text to change the formatting.

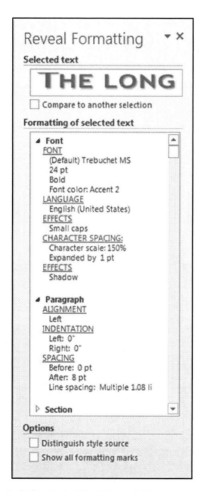

Exhibit 1-1: The Reveal Formatting task pane

Comparing formatting

You can use the Reveal Formatting task pane to compare the text formatting of two selections. To do so, verify that the first selection appears in the Selected text box. Then, in the Reveal Formatting task pane, check "Compare to another selection" to display a second Selected text box. Finally, in the document, select the text to be compared. The result of the comparison is shown in the Formatting differences box.

Do it!   **A-1:   Using the Reveal Formatting task pane**

The files for this activity are in Student Data folder **Unit 1\Topic A**.

Here's how	Here's why
1 Open Cookbook1	
Save the document as **My cookbook1**	(In the current topic folder.) Some changes have been made to one of the page headings. You want to compare the heading with another and format them similarly.
2 Move to page 3	
Select the heading **The long history of spices**	
3 Press (SHIFT) + (F1)	To open the Reveal Formatting task pane, which displays the formatting of the selected text.
4 In the Reveal Formatting task pane, check **Compare to another selection**	You'll compare the "Contents" heading with the heading on page 3.
5 Move to page 2	
Select the heading **Contents**	You'll observe the differences in formatting and then format them to match.
Observe the Formatting differences box	
	The differences between the two selections appear in the box. The first selection has a font size of 24 pt and uses small caps, while the second selection is 22 pt and doesn't use small caps. In addition, the first selection uses the shadow effect, and the second doesn't.

6 In the Reveal Formatting task pane, click **Font**, as shown

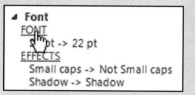

To open the Font dialog box.

From the Size list, select **24**

Check **Small caps**

Click **OK**

To close the dialog box. Word updates the Reveal Formatting task pane to reflect the font and effect changes.

7 Click **Effects**

(In the Reveal Formatting task pane.) To open the Format Text Effects task pane.

Click

The Text Effects icon.

Under Shadow, from the Presets gallery, select the indicated option

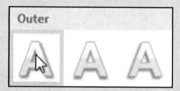

Word updates the Reveal Formatting task pane to indicate that there are now no formatting differences.

Close the Format Text Effects task pane

8 Close the Reveal Formatting task pane

9 Update and close the document

Topic B: Working with styles

This topic covers the following Microsoft Office Specialist exam objectives for exam 77-418: Word 2013.

#	Objective
2.2	**Format text and paragraphs**
2.2.9	Add styles to text
2.2.11	Modify existing style attributes

This topic covers the following Microsoft Office Specialist exam objectives for exam 77-419: Word Expert 2013.

#	Objective
1.1	**Manage multiple documents**
1.1.4	Copy styles from template to template
1.1.5	Demonstrate how to use the style organizer
1.3	**Manage document changes**
1.3.4	Resolve multi-document style conflicts
2.2	**Apply advanced styles**
2.2.1	Create custom styles
2.2.2	Create custom styles
2.2.3	Create character-specific styles
2.2.4	Assign keyboard shortcuts to styles

Explanation

A *style* is a named set of formatting options (font, font size, font color, effects, and so on) that define the appearance of recurring text elements, such as headings or body text. By using a style, you can apply several formats in one step. Using styles helps to maintain formatting consistency.

Applying styles

You can apply a style to selected text by selecting the desired style from the Styles gallery on the Home tab, shown in Exhibit 1-2. Word provides several built-in styles. For example, you can apply the Heading 1 style to format selected text as a heading. When you create a document, all text uses the Normal style unless you apply a different style to it or format it manually.

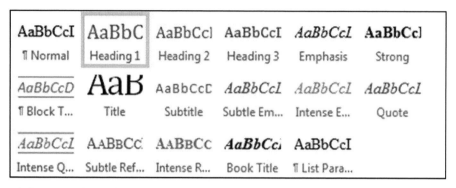

Exhibit 1-2: The Styles gallery

Do it!

B-1:   Applying a style

The files for this activity are in Student Data folder **Unit 1\Topic B**.

Here's how	Here's why
1 Open Cookbook2	
Save the document as **My cookbook2**	In the current topic folder.
2 At the bottom of page 2, click in **The long history of spices**	You don't have to select the entire heading.
On the Home tab, click **Heading 1**	(In the Styles group.) To apply the Heading 1 style to the page heading. This style formats the text as blue, bold, 16pt Cambria.
3 Click in the subheading **Introduction**	You'll apply a style to this text.
4 In the gallery, select **Heading 2**	To apply the Heading 2 style to the subheading.
5 Update the document	

Creating styles by example

You might have formatted some text by using a combination of options that you want to apply to other text. If you plan to use the same combination of formats repeatedly, you can create a style based on the formatting of selected text.

To create a style based on selected text:

1 Select the text on which you want to base the new style.

2 Display the Styles gallery and choose Create a Style to open the Create New Style from Formatting dialog box.

3 Edit the Name box to name the style.

4 Click Modify to display formatting options, as shown in Exhibit 1-3.

5 Click OK to create the style, which will now be available in the Styles gallery.

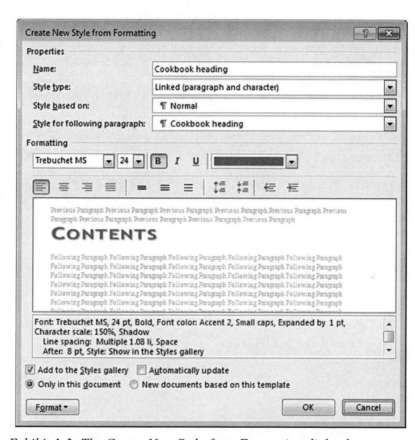

Exhibit 1-3: The Create New Style from Formatting dialog box

Basing styles on other styles

Another way to create a style is to base it on an existing style. The new style inherits the formatting of the style it's based on, and any additional formats you select either replace or are added to the inherited options.

To base a new style on an existing style:

1 Display the Styles gallery and choose Create a Style.

2 Click Modify.

3 From the Style based on list, select an existing style.

4 Select any other formatting option you want to apply.

5 Click OK to create the style.

B-2: Creating styles

Here's how	Here's why
1 On page 1, select the heading **Contents**	
2 Display the Styles gallery and choose **Create a Style**	(On the Home tab.) To open the Create New Style from Formatting dialog box.
Edit the Name box to read **Cookbook heading**	
Click **OK**	To create the style. It appears in the Styles gallery. You'll now apply the new style to other headings in the document.
3 At the bottom of page 2, place the insertion point in **The long history of spices**	
On the Home tab, select the **Cookbook heading** style	
	To apply the style to the text.
4 On page 3, select the heading **The medicinal use of spices**	
5 Display the Styles gallery and choose **Create a Style**	
Edit the Name box to read **Cookbook subhead**	
Click **OK**	
6 On page 2, apply the **Cookbook subhead** style to the text Introduction	Select the text. Then, on the Home tab, select the style.
	Next, you'll base a new style on an existing style.
7 Move to page 4 and select the heading **Bay leaf**	This text has the Heading 1 style applied to it.
8 Open the Create New Style from Formatting dialog box	Display the Styles gallery and choose Create a Style.
Edit the Name box to read **Spice heading**	
Click **Modify**	To display formatting options.

9 From the Style based on list,
   select **Cookbook heading**

   From the Font Color gallery,
   select the indicated color

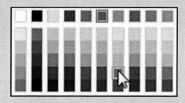

Olive Green, Accent 3, Darker 25%.

Click **OK**   To apply the style. It uses all of the formatting
                                applied to the Cookbook heading style, but with
                                a different font color.

10 Apply the **Spice heading** style   Click in the text and select Spice heading in the
    to the following text: Styles gallery.

    On page 5: **Cinnamon**

    On page 6: **Cloves**

    On page 7: **Coriander**

    On page 8: **Cumin**

    On page 9: **Nutmeg**

    On page 10: **Pepper**

    On page 11: **Star anise** and
    Turmeric

11 Update the document

Managing styles

Explanation   One of the advantages of using styles is the ease with which you can make global
changes. For example, if you change any of a style's properties, then all text formatted
with that style automatically inherits the new properties. If your document contains
multiple headings, subheadings, and other elements to which you've applied styles, this
feature can be a big time-saver.

You can use the Styles task pane, shown in Exhibit 1-4, to create, modify, and apply
styles. You can either create a style from scratch or modify an existing style and save it
with a new name. To open the Styles task pane, click the Styles group Dialog Box
Launcher (on the Home tab.)

To apply a style by using the Styles task pane, first select the text you want to format.
Then, in the Styles list, select the desired style.

Exhibit 1-4: The Styles task pane

To modify a style, use the Modify Style dialog box. To open the Modify Style dialog box, do either of the following:

- In the Styles task pane, point to the name of the style you want to modify. Click the down-arrow to the right of the style name and choose Modify.

- In the Styles task pane, click the Manage Styles button to open the Manage Styles dialog box. Select a style and click Modify.

In the Modify Style dialog box, you can adjust the style's formatting just as you would in the Create New Style from Formatting dialog box. In addition to font attributes, you can include other formatting options in a style. For example, you can use styles to apply paragraph, tab, and border formatting to text.

To select additional formatting options for a new style:

1   In the Modify Style dialog box (or in the Create New Style from Formatting dialog box), click Format to show the additional options. For example, to assign a keyboard shortcut to a style, click Format and choose Shortcut key.

2   Select the kind of formatting you want to change.

3   Set the desired options, and then click OK to close the dialog box.

4   Click OK to save the settings.

Overriding styles

There might be times when you want to change the formatting of text after applying a style to it. For example, after applying the Heading 1 style, you might decide to increase the heading font to 20 pt and change the case to small caps. When you manually format text that already has a style applied to it, you are *overriding* the style; the override is local and does not affect any other text with that style applied. When you override a style, the Styles task pane lists a new style entry, consisting of the original style name followed by the additional formatting, such as "Cookbook heading + Not Small Caps," as shown in Exhibit 1-5.

Exhibit 1-5: The Cookbook heading style, showing a style override

You can have Word update a style automatically every time you apply manual formatting to text with that style applied. This feature controls whether styles can be overridden. To enable automatic updating of styles, open the Modify Style dialog box for that style and check Automatically update. When enabled, any formatting you add will modify the style's global definition, rather than overriding the formatting locally.

Deleting styles

You can delete a style from a document by using the Styles task pane. To do so, point to the name of the style you want to delete, click the down-arrow to the right of the style name, and choose Delete. When you delete a paragraph style, text that has been formatted with that style will revert to the Normal paragraph style.

Do it! **B-3: Modifying styles**

Here's how	Here's why
1 Scroll through the document	To observe that the text all flows together. You want to insert a page break wherever a heading is used.
2 Click the Styles group Dialog Box Launcher	To open the Styles task pane.
In the Styles task pane, click	(The Manage Styles button.) To open the Manage Styles dialog box.
3 From the "Select a style to edit" list, select **Cookbook heading**	Scroll to the top of the list.
Click **Modify**	To open the Modify Style dialog box.
4 Click **Format** and choose **Paragraph...**	To open the Paragraph dialog box.
Click the **Line and Page Breaks** tab	
Check **Page break before**	
5 Click **OK**	To close the Paragraph dialog box.
6 Click **Format** and choose **Shortcut key...**	To open the Customize Keyboard dialog box.
Place the insertion point in the Press new shortcut key box	
Press (CTRL) + (S) + (C)	Press new shortcut key: Ctrl+S,C To assign the keyboard shortcut.
From the Save changes in list, select **My cookbook2**	To save the shortcut key in the current document, rather than in the Normal template.
7 Click **Assign**	
Click **Close**	
8 Click **OK**	To close the Modify Style dialog box.
Click **OK**	To close the Manage Styles dialog box.

9	Scroll to page 3	The headings on pages 2 and 3 use the Cookbook heading style.
	Scroll to page 5	The Bay leaf heading uses the Spice heading style; because you specified that this style is based on the Cookbook heading style, the Spice heading style inherits its formatting, so there's a page break before the heading.
	Scroll to page 13	All of the spice headings now include page breaks. However, the recipe headings do not.
10	At the bottom of page 13, apply the **Spice heading** style to **Spicy Buzzard Wings**	Observe that the page breaks above the recipe name after you apply the style.
11	Apply the **Spice heading** style to the remaining recipe names	Montego Bay Jerk Chicken, Big D Veggie Chile, Crème Brulee, and Wasabi Pork Tenderloin
12	On page 2, select **Contents**	You've applied the Cookbook heading style to this text, but you want to change its formatting without affecting any other text that uses the same style.
13	Press CTRL + D	To open the Font dialog box.
	On the Font tab, clear **Small caps**	
	On the **Advanced** tab, from the Spacing list, select **Normal**	
	Click **OK**	To close the dialog box.
14	Observe the Styles task pane	A description of the additional formatting appears next to the Main Heading style to indicate that you've overridden it.
15	Update the document	

Character styles

A character style is similar to a paragraph style, except that a character style applies only to selected text and doesn't include paragraph formats. (A paragraph style can include both character and paragraph formats.) You can use a character style to format specific text without affecting the other text in the paragraph.

To create a character style:

1 Open the Create New Style from Formatting dialog box.
2 Name the style.
3 From the Style type list, select Character.
4 Select the desired formatting options.
5 Click OK.

B-4: Creating a character style

Here's how	Here's why
1 At the top of page 14, select **Category**	Below the text "Spicy Buzzard Wings."
2 In the Styles task pane, click [icon]	The New Style button.
3 Name the style **Label**	
From the Style type list, select **Character**	So that the style's formatting will be applied to selected characters, rather than to entire paragraphs.
Format the text as bold, with a white color	
4 Click **Format** and choose **Border...**	To open the Borders and Shading dialog box.
5 Click the **Shading** tab	
From the Fill list, select the Olive Green, Accent 3, Darker 50% color	
6 Click **OK**	To close the Borders and Shading dialog box.
Click **OK**	
7 Select the word **Yield**	Under "Spicy Buzzard Wings."
In the Styles task pane, select **Label**	To apply the character style.
8 Update and close the document	

Copying styles

Explanation

After you create a style that is stored in a single document, you might want to copy it to other files or templates. To copy a style between files:

1   Open both the file containing the style to be copied and the destination file.

2   Activate the document containing the style, and open the Manage Styles dialog box.

3   Click Import/Export to open the Organizer dialog box with the Styles Items tab active, as shown in Exhibit 1-6.

4   From the "Styles available in" list on the left (or right) side, select the file or template containing the style you want to copy.

5   From the "Styles available in" list on the right (or left) side, select the file or template to which you want to copy the style. If the file is not available in the list, click Close File and then click Open File to display the Open dialog box. From the Open dialog box, open the file you want.

6   Select the style to be copied and click Copy. (If the style already exists, Word will ask whether you want to overwrite the existing style.)

7   Click Close to close the Organizer dialog box.

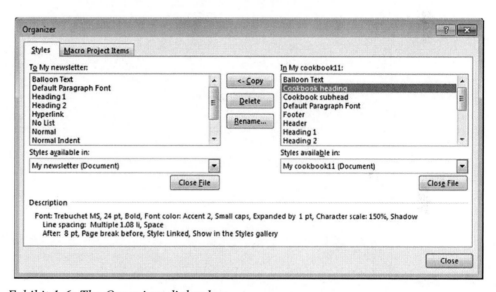

Exhibit 1-6: The Organizer dialog box

Do it!   ## B-5:   Exporting a style

The files for this activity are in Student Data folder **Unit 1\Topic B**.

Here's how	Here's why
1 Open Newsletter	
Save the document as **My newsletter**	
2 In the Styles task pane, click	To open the Manage Styles dialog box.
3 Click **Import/Export**	To open the Organizer dialog box.
4 On the right side of the Organizer, click **Close File**	The button name changes to Open File.
5 Click **Open File**	The Open dialog box appears.
Navigate to the current topic folder	
From the file types list, select **Word Documents**	
Select **My cookbook 2** and click **Open**	
6 On the right side of the Organizer, select **Cookbook heading**	
7 Click **Copy**	To copy the style from My cookbook2 to My newsletter.
Click **Close**	To close the Organizer dialog box.
8 Observe the Styles task pane	The Cookbook heading style now appears.
9 Update and close My newsletter	
Update and close My cookbook2	

Topic C: Working with outlines

This topic covers the following Microsoft Office Specialist exam objectives for exam 77-419: Word Expert 2013.

#	Objective
2.3	**Apply advanced ordering and grouping**
2.3.1	Create outlines
2.3.2	Promote sections in outlines

Explanation

An *outline* provides a helpful way to view the main sections of a document. In Word, an outline consists of headings and subheadings that are formatted with an outline level. Outlines also help you with navigating in long documents because they enable you to collapse and expand text to view different levels.

Using styles to create an outline

When you format a document with Word's predefined heading or subheading styles, Word automatically creates an outline. You can switch to Outline view by clicking the Outline button on the Views tab. When you switch to this view, the Outlining tab becomes available on the ribbon. This tab has three groups: Outline Tools, Master Document, and Close.

To create an outline, you can apply the default styles Heading 1, Heading 2, and Heading 3 to text to create Level 1, Level 2, and Level 3 outline levels, as shown in Exhibit 1-7. You can also use the Outline Tools group, shown in Exhibit 1-8, to set and manipulate outline levels.

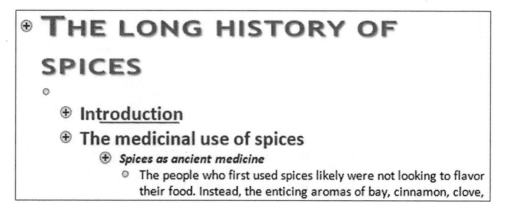

Exhibit 1-7: A document in Outline view, showing Level 1, Level 2, Level 3, and Body Text levels

Exhibit 1-8: The Outline Tools group on the Outlining tab

The following table describes some of the commands in the Outline Tools group.

Button	Shortcut	Description
⟪		Promotes the selected text to the Heading 1 style (Level 1 outline level).
←	ALT + SHIFT + ←	Promotes the selected text to the next highest outline level. If the text is already subordinate to an outline level, that text is promoted to the level to which it is subordinate.
→	ALT + SHIFT + →	Demotes the selected text to the next lowest outline level. If the text is already subordinate to an outline level, it is demoted to the next level below that to which it is subordinate.
⟫		Demotes the selected text to Body text.
▲	ALT + SHIFT + ↑	Moves the selected paragraph up in the outline, without changing its outline level.
▼	ALT + SHIFT + ↓	Moves the selected paragraph down in the outline, without changing its outline level.
✦	ALT + +	If collapsed, expands the selected outline level.
▬	ALT + _	If expanded, collapses the selected outline level.

Formatting styles for an outline

When you apply an outline level to text in Outline view, Word assigns that text a corresponding style. You can change the formatting for these styles just as you would for a style you created. For example, if you want all Level 1 headings to use the font Trebuchet MS, you can format the Heading 1 style to use that font. To change the formatting for an outline level, select the desired options in the corresponding style's Modify Style dialog box.

Alternatively, you can create a style, specify its outline level, and apply it to text to create an outline. For example, if you had a style named Cookbook heading, you could specify that it uses outline Level 1. Then, when you apply that style to a heading, it will automatically be formatted as Level 1.

To set the outline level for a style:

1 In the Styles task pane, click the Manage Styles button.

2 Select the style to which you want to assign an outline level, and click Modify.

3 Click Format and choose Paragraph.

4 Select an option from the Outline level list.

- For the Normal style, the default level is Body text. Any style based on Normal (the "based on" default) will also use the Body text level for outlining.

- For Heading 1, the default level is Level 1; for Heading 2, it's Level 2; and for Heading 3, it's Level 3.

- There are 10 outline levels: Body text, and Level 1 through Level 9.

5 Click OK.

Do it!

C-1:   Specifying outline levels

The files for this activity are in Student Data folder **Unit 1\Topic C**.

Here's how	Here's why
1 Open Cookbook3	
Save the document as **My cookbook3**	(In the current topic folder.) This document contains styles that you'll use to create an outline.
2 Open the Styles task pane	(If necessary.) Click the Styles group Dialog Box Launcher.
3 On the View tab, click **Outline**	To view the document as an outline. The entire document currently uses the Body Text outline level. You'll specify that certain styles use other outline levels.
4 In the Styles task pane, click 🗒	To open the Manage Styles dialog box.
On the Edit tab, select **Cookbook heading** and click **Modify**	
Click **Format** and choose **Paragraph...**	
On the Indents and Spacing tab, from the Outline level list, select **Level 1**	
Click **OK** twice	To return to the Manage Styles dialog box.

5	Apply the **Level 2** outline level to the Cookbook subhead style	Select it and click Modify. Then click Format and choose Paragraph. From the Outline level list, select Level 2. Click OK twice.
	Click **OK**	To close the Manage Styles dialog box.
6	Scroll down	

⊕ **THE LONG HISTORY OF SPICES**

○

⊕ **Introduction**

○ You already know that having a well-stocked spice rack or cabinet is

		To see that the text with the styles you modified now use the outline levels you specified.
7	Scroll down to The spice trade	This heading doesn't use a style.
	In the Styles task pane, select **Cookbook subhead**	To apply the style, which also applies an outline level.
8	Scroll to the top of the document and place the insertion point within **A word from the chairman**	You can specify an outline level without modifying the style applied to the text.
	On the Outlining tab, from the Outline Level list, select **Level 1**	← Level 1 ▾ →
9	Scroll down and select the text **Spices as ancient medicine**	⊕ **The medicinal use of spices** ○ *Spices as ancient medicine*
	On the Outlining tab, click ←	To promote its outline level. Because the text above it is Level 2, it is "promoted" to Level 2.
	On the Outlining tab, click →	To demote it to Level 3.
10	Scroll down and select the text **Spices as modern medicine**	The text above it is Level 3, so promoting this text will make it Level 3 as well.
	On the Outlining tab, click ←	
11	Under The spice trade, make the text beginning with "A funny thing happened" Level 3	Either click the Demote button, or select Level 3 from the Outline Level list.
12	Update the document	

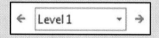

Organizing outlines

Explanation

You can use Outline view to easily rearrange an outlined document. Outlining below text indicates that there is additional text under the level heading, as shown in Exhibit 1-9. Double-click the plus sign to collapse the subordinate text under a level heading, and double-click it again to expand the text.

When you point to a plus sign in an outline, the pointer changes to a four-headed arrow, indicating that you can move the outline level. To do so, drag the plus sign to where you want the outline level—as well as any subordinate text—to appear in the outline. Alternatively, in the Outline Tools group, click Show First Line Only to show only the first line of each paragraph. Also, you can choose which levels to show by selecting an option from the Show Level list.

⊕ **THE LONG HISTORY OF SPICES**
    ⊕ **Introduction**
    ⊕ **The medicinal use of spices**
        ⊕ *Spices as ancient medicine*
        ⊕ *Spices as modern medicine*
    ⊕ **The spice trade**
        ⊕ *A funny thing happened on the way to the Spice Lands...*

Exhibit 1-9: A document with outline levels collapsed

The Navigation pane

In addition to dragging outline levels in the document, you can use the Navigation pane to view and arrange a document outline. The Navigation pane displays document headings by outline level, as shown in Exhibit 1-10. To display this pane, click the View tab and check Navigation Pane in the Show group. To view an outline of document headings, click Headings.

The Navigation pane can be helpful for navigating through a long document. As you move the insertion point in the document, corresponding headings on each page are highlighted in the Navigation pane. You can also click the headings in the Navigation pane to go directly to them in the document.

To rearrange headings in the Navigation pane, drag a heading to where you want it in the pane. A blue line indicates where the heading and the text below it will appear.

Note: To use the Navigation pane to browse headings, the document must contain heading styles or styles with outline levels defined.

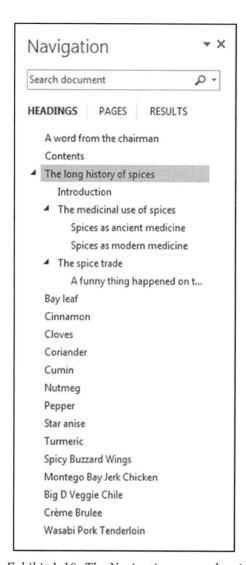

Exhibit 1-10: The Navigation pane, showing document headings

Do it!

C-2: Organizing an outline

Here's how	Here's why
1 On page 3, double-click the plus sign to the left of "Spices as ancient medicine"	To collapse the text subordinate to that heading.
2 Double-click the plus sign to the left of "The medicinal use of spices"	To collapse the headings and text subordinate to that heading.
3 On the Outlining tab, from the Show Level list, select **Level 3**	To view only Levels 1, 2, and 3 of the outline. The Body Text level is hidden.

4 Drag the plus sign to the left of "The spice trade" so that it's above "The medicinal use of spices," as shown

In the screenshot below, notice the position of the mouse pointer (the vertical, double-headed arrow). This is the position you're dragging to.

⊕ **Introduction**

⇕ ⊕ **The medicinal use of spices**

⊕ *Spices as ancient medicine*
⊕ *Spices as modern medicine*

⊕ **The spice trade**

⊕ *A funny thing happened on the way to the Spice Lands...*

5 On the Outlining tab, click **Close Outline View**

To close Outline view. You can also organize an outline by using the Navigation pane.

6 On the View tab, check **Navigation Pane**

To open the Navigation task pane.

In the Navigation pane, click **Headings**

(If necessary.) To see an outline of your document's headings.

7 In the Navigation task pane, click as shown

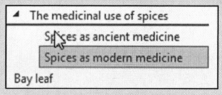

To go to that heading in the document.

8 Drag the heading as shown

To move the heading and its subordinate text in the outline.

9 Close the Navigation task pane

Close the Styles task pane

10 Update and close the document

Unit summary: Styles and outlines

Topic A   In this topic, you learned how to examine text formatting and compare the formatting of two selections by using the **Reveal Formatting** task pane.

Topic B   In this topic, you applied a **style** to some text. Then you learned how to create a style by example and how to base one style on another. You also modified a style by using the **Manage Styles** dialog box, and you learned how to override a style. Finally, you created a **character style**.

Topic C   In this topic, you used styles to create an **outline**. Then you used Outline view and the Navigation pane to **organize** an outline.

Independent practice activity

In this activity, you'll compare the styles of two selections and make them match. Then you'll create a style, apply it, use it to create a document outline, and view the outline.

The files for this activity are in Student Data folder **Unit 1\Unit summary**.

1 Open Newsletter text and save it as **My newsletter text**.

2 Use the Reveal Formatting task pane to examine the formatting of the heading on page 1. (*Hint:* Press Shift+F1.)

3 Use the Reveal Formatting task pane to format the heading on page 1 by using the same formatting options that are used for the heading on page 2.

4 Create a style named **Page heading**, based on the format of the heading on page 1.

5 Set the Page heading style to use outline Level 1.

6 Apply the Page heading style to the headings on pages 2, 3, 4, 5, 7, and 8.

7 View the document in Outline view, and then return to Print Layout view.

8 Display the Navigation pane, if necessary.

9 In the Navigation pane, move the Spices of the Month section below the Outlander Spice Collection section.

10 Close any open panes.

11 Update and close the document.

Review questions

1 What keys do you press to open the Reveal Formatting task pane?

2 How do you use the Reveal Formatting task pane to compare the formatting of two selections?

3 What are some advantages of using styles?

4 What style is applied to a new, blank document by default?

5 You've created a section-heading style named "Appendix Heading." You want this style to have the same formatting as the Heading 1 style, but you want the new style to make text red. How can you do this without manually specifying every style setting?

6 How can you use Word's predefined styles to create an outline?

7 If you want to create an outline from a document that uses custom styles, how can you do so?

8 How can you view and organize a document outline in Print Layout view?

Unit 2
Table formatting

Complete this unit, and you'll know how to:

A Change table borders, apply shading to cells, and apply styles to tables.

B Sort data in a table, split a table, repeat a header row on multiple pages, and enter a formula in a table.

Topic A: Table design options

This topic covers the following Microsoft Office Specialist exam objectives for exam 77-418: Word 2013.

#	Objective
3.2	**Modify a table**
3.2.1	Apply styles to tables

Explanation

After you've created a table, you can apply borders and shading to highlight cells, rows, columns, or the entire table. By using the formatting options on the Table Tools | Design tab, you can apply borders of different widths and styles, and you can apply borders to different areas of a table. You can also apply different shading to selected cells.

Table borders

To apply table borders, first select options the Table Tools | Design tab, in the Borders group, shown in Exhibit 2-1:

- From the Border Styles gallery, select a border style.
- From the Line Style gallery, select a line style.
- From the Line Weight list, select a thickness.
- From the Pen Color gallery, select a color.

The Border Painter is automatically activated when you specify a selection in the Borders group. To use it, drag across a table border to apply the formatting. This works similarly to the Borders menu, but you might find it easier to "paint" the formatting directly on the table.

To use the Borders menu, select one or more cells or an entire table, then specify how you want to apply the border.

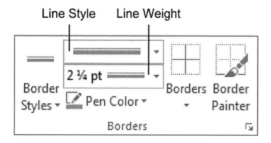

Exhibit 2-1: The Borders group

Border Sampler

In the Border Styles gallery, you can select Border Sampler to sample an existing border from a table. When the Border Sampler is active, simply click a table border to sample it; the Border Painter then becomes active, and you can drag to apply the sampled border as desired.

Do it!

A-1: Changing table borders

The files for this activity are in Student Data folder **Unit 2\Topic A**.

Here's how	Here's why
1 Open Tables1	
Save the document as **My tables1**	In the current topic folder.
2 Select the indicated cells	

MD		Baltimore	Prestige Market	112
		Bethesda	Prestige Market	175
		Rockville	Mediterranean Gourmet	80

3 Click the **Design** tab	
In the Borders group, display the Borders gallery and select **Inside Borders**	To deselect the option, removing the inside borders from the selection.
4 Format the borders as shown	

MD	Baltimore	Prestige Market	112
	Bethesda	Prestige Market	175
	Rockville	Mediterranean Gourmet	80
NJ	Atlantic City	Roma	125
	Cherry Hill	Patterson's Grocers	180
	Trenton	Roma	75
NY	Albany	Prestige Market	95
	Buffalo	Mediterranean Gourmet	60
	New York	Patterson's Grocers	215
	New York	Village Gourmet Bakery	230
PA	Harrisburg	Patterson's Grocers	140
	Philadelphia	Patterson's Grocers	165
	Pittsburgh	Patterson's Grocers	136
VA	Charlottesville	Roma	120
	Fairfax	Mediterranean Gourmet	110

Select the rows for each state and remove the inside borders.

5 In the top table, select the header row

    Display the Border Styles gallery and select the indicated style

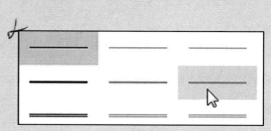

    (Single solid line, 1 1/2 pt, Accent 2.) Word specifies options in the other lists in the Borders group based on this style.

    From the Line Style gallery, select the indicated style

    From the Line Weight list, select **2 1/4 pt**

6 Drag as shown to apply the border

State	Sales Manager	City	Store Location	Projected Revenues (in $ thousands)
MD		Baltimore	Prestige Market	112

    Press (ESC)   To deselect the Border Painter.

7 Update the document

Cell shading

Explanation

You might want to highlight some sections of a table to visually differentiate them from other sections, as shown in Exhibit 2-2. You can apply shading to do so. You can apply shading to the entire table or to specific cells. First select the cells you want to shade. Then, on the Table Tools | Design tab, in the Table Styles group, select a color in the Shading gallery.

State	Sales Manager	City	Store Location	Projected Revenues (in $ thousands)
MD		Baltimore	Prestige Market	112
		Bethesda	Prestige Market	175
		Rockville	Mediterranean Gourmet	80

Exhibit 2-2: Shaded cells in a table

Do it!

A-2:   Shading table cells

Here's how	Here's why
1 Select the cells in the header row	
2 On the Design tab, display the Shading gallery and select the indicated color	Orange, Accent 2, Lighter 60%.
3 Select the cells below the Projected Revenues heading	
4 In the Shading gallery, select the indicated color	Green, Accent 6, Lighter 60%.
5 Update the document	

Table styles

You can apply styles to tables by using the Table Styles gallery on the Table Tools | Design tab. Word provides several style formats you can use to display information in different kinds of tables. For example, you might want to highlight specific columns or rows, or you might want to shade alternate columns or rows to make reading the data easier. You can do this manually, but you might also be able to use one of Word's table styles.

To apply a style to a table, first place the insertion point in the table. Then, on the Table Tools | Design tab, select a style from the Table Styles gallery.

Customizing table styles

If the styles in the Table Styles gallery don't quite work for the data in your table, you can quickly select options that might correct the problem. For example, you might want to select a style because you like the shading; however, maybe you don't want the first column to be formatted differently from the rest of the table, which that style might do by default. In the Table Style Options group, you can select from several options for customizing a table style.

Do it!

A-3:   Applying table styles

Here's how	Here's why
1 Click any cell in the top table	
2 Click the **Design** tab	
3 In the Table Styles group, point to any table style	(Do not click the mouse button). As you point to each style, the document displays the resulting table format in the document window.
4 Click as shown	(The More button.) To expand the gallery.
In the gallery, select the Grid Table 5 Dark - Accent 2 style	(Use the ScreenTips to find this style.) You like the shading but want to adjust how it's applied.
5 In the Table Style Options group, clear **First Column**	
Check **Last Column**	
Clear **Banded Rows**	
6 Update the document	

Using the Modify Style dialog box

Explanation

To customize a table style even further, you can use the Modify Style dialog box. Expand the Table Styles gallery and choose Modify Table Style to open the Modify Style dialog box, shown in Exhibit 2-3.

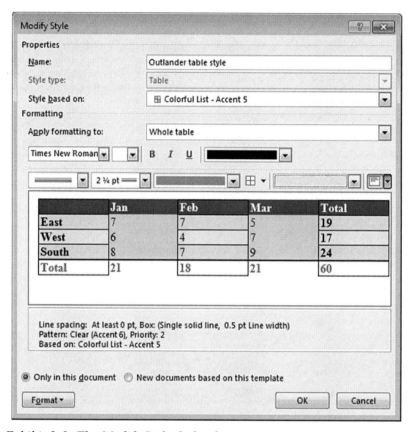

Exhibit 2-3: The Modify Style dialog box

Do it!   **A-4: Modifying a table style**

Here's how	Here's why
1 Click in the bottom table	
2 In the Table Style gallery, choose **Modify Table Style...**	To open the Modify Style dialog box.
3 Edit the Name box to read **Outlander table style**	
From the "Style based on" list, select **Colorful List - Accent 5**	You'll modify some of the default settings.
4 Under Formatting, from the "Apply formatting to" list, select **Header row**	
In the Fill Color gallery, select the dark green color	Green, Accent 6, Darker 50%.
5 From the "Apply formatting to" list, select **Whole table**	
In the Fill Color gallery, select the light green color	Green, Accent 6, Lighter 80%.
6 Click **OK**	To save the new style and apply it to the selected table.
7 In the Table Style Options group, clear **First Column** and **Banded Rows**	
8 Update and close the document	

Topic B: Table data

This topic covers the following Microsoft Office Specialist exam objectives for exam 77-418: Word 2013.

#	Objective
3.1	**Create a table**
3.1.6	Set a table title
3.2	**Modify a table**
3.2.3	Sort table data
3.2.5	Demonstrate how to apply formulas to a table

Explanation

Tables in Word have some of the same functionality as tables in Excel. For example, you can sort data, and you can insert equations in table cells. For more complex operations, however, you should use a spreadsheet program like Excel.

Sorting data in a table

You can use the Sort command to organize table information in a particular order. To do so, first select the rows to be organized. Then, on the Table Tools | Layout tab, click Sort to open the Sort dialog box, shown in Exhibit 2-4. By default, the selected data is sorted alphabetically in ascending order. You can also sort numerically or chronologically.

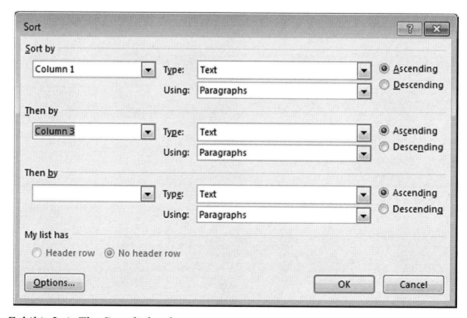

Exhibit 2-4: The Sort dialog box

Do it!

B-1: Sorting table data

The files for this activity are in Student Data folder **Unit 2\Topic B**.

Here's how	Here's why
1 Open Sales report	
Save the document as **My sales report**	In the current topic folder.
2 Observe the table data	You want to organize the table by region, and then by sales in each region.
3 Select all of the rows below the header rows	The first row is Ginger.
On the Layout tab, click **Sort**	To open the Sort dialog box.
4 From the Sort by list, select **Column 2**	To have the table rows sorted initially by region.
From the Then by list, select **Column 3**	To have the table rows within each region sorted by sales.
Observe the Type list	To see that Word recognizes this column contains numerical data.
Click **OK**	To sort the table data.
5 Update the document	

Repeating a header row across multiple pages

Explanation

When you have a table that spans multiple pages, you probably want the header row to appear at the top of each page. In Word, the *header row* is the first row in a table, and typically it contains descriptive headings for the data in each column. If the header row appears at the top of each page, people reading the table don't have to flip back to the first page to determine which column they're viewing. At the same time, if you add or remove rows or format the table differently, you'll still want the header to appear at the top of each page, rather than to re-flow with the rest of the table.

To do this, make sure that the header you want to use is the top row of the table. Then, with that row selected, click the Table Tools | Layout tab and click Repeat Header Rows in the Data group. You can also open the Table Properties dialog box, click the Row tab, and check "Repeat as header row at the top of each page."

Splitting tables

You might be working with one table that you want to split into two. For example, you might want to sort different sections of a table or show sections separately, with text in between. To split a table:

1   Place the insertion point where you want to split the table. The selected row will be the first row of the new table.

2   On the Table Tools | Layout tab, click Split Table.

Do it!   **B-2:   Repeating the header row**

Here's how	Here's why
1 Scroll to examine the table	The data continues onto a second page. You want the header to appear at the top of each new page that contains this table.
Return to the top of the document	
2 Place the insertion point in the empty row below "Sales report"	You'll split the table so that the next row is the header row. Word automatically identifies the top row of a table as the header.
On the Layout tab, click **Split Table**	
Delete the empty row	Select it and press Backspace.
3 Place the insertion point in the header row of the second table	(If necessary.) The header row contains the Product, Region, Prior year, and Current year cells.
4 On the Layout tab, click **Repeat Header Rows**	In the Data group.
5 Move to page 2	The header appears at the top of the page. If you added rows to or removed rows from the first page of the table, the header would still appear at the top of this page, as long as the table continued onto it.
6 Update the document	

Using the Formula dialog box

You can perform various calculations in rows and columns by using formulas. A *formula* is used to perform arithmetic operations, such as calculating an average or a sum. You can also copy formulas from one cell to another in a table.

You can create formulas by using the Formula dialog box, shown in Exhibit 2-5. To open the Formula dialog box, click the Table Tools | Design tab and click Formula in the Data group. In the Formula dialog box:

- A formula is always preceded by an equal sign (=).

- From the Number format list, you can select the format in which you want the result displayed, such as currency or a percentage.

- From the Paste function list, select the function you want to use in the formula. A *function* is a built-in formula used to perform mathematical calculations. For example, the SUM function adds the numbers in the selected cells.

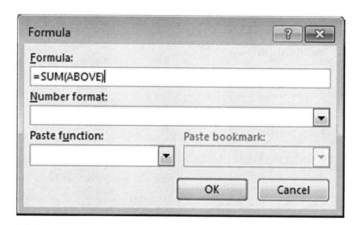

Exhibit 2-5: The Formula dialog box

In Word documents, formulas are treated as fields. When information is subject to change, a *field* is used as a placeholder for that information. For example, a formula that totals a column of numbers is based on the values in the column. If any number in the column changes, the formula needs to reflect the change. In such situations, fields provide the best way to store and display dynamic information.

Calculating totals in rows and columns

Use the SUM function to calculate totals in rows and columns. If the insertion point is in a table containing a series of numbers, the SUM function appears in the Formula dialog box by default. If the insertion point is placed below a cell containing a number, the Formula box will contain =SUM(ABOVE), which adds the numbers in the column. By default, the formula result will have the same formatting as the numbers used in the calculation.

Do it!   **B-3:   Entering a formula in a table**

Here's how	Here's why
1 Add a new row at the end of the table	On page 2.
Under the Turmeric cell, type **TOTALS**	(see table below)
2 Press ⌈TAB⌋ twice	To place the insertion point in the empty cell in the Prior year column.
On the Table Tools | Layout tab, click **Formula**	(In the Data group.) To open the Formula dialog box. You'll use the default formula.
Click **OK**	To insert a field that calculates the sum of the cells above the selected cell.
3 Press ⌈TAB⌋	To place the insertion point in the empty cell in the Current year column.
Insert a sum formula	Click Formula, then click OK.
4 Update and close the document	

Oregano	West
Turmeric	West
TOTALS	

Unit summary: Table formatting

Topic A   In this topic, you changed a table's **borders** and applied **shading** to table cells. You also applied and modified **table styles**.

Topic B   In this topic, you used the Sort dialog box to **sort data** in a table. You also learned how to split a table and how to repeat a **header row** on multiple pages. Finally, you learned how to enter **formulas** in a table.

Independent practice activity

In this activity, you'll format a table by applying a border and shading selected cells. Then you'll sort the table data, insert a formula, and format the header row across multiple pages.

1 Open Employee info and save it as **My employee info**.

2 Apply an outside border to the header row (containing the Employee ID, Name, etc. columns) that is a solid black line, 1½ pt thick.

3 Shade the header row with a light blue color.

4 Sort the table by earnings, starting with the highest salary. (*Hint:* Remember to select the cells you want to sort before opening the Sort dialog box.)

5 Insert a new row at the bottom of the table.

6 In the rightmost cell of the last row, insert a formula that calculates the total of the salaries shown in the column.

7 Split the table so that the row containing the column headers (Employee ID, Name, etc.) appears at the top of a table separate from the cells containing "Outlander Spices" and "Employee Information." (*Hint:* The employee data should all appear in one table, separate from the title, with the column headers in the top row. Delete any unnecessary rows from either table.)

8 Format the second table (containing the employee data) to include a header row. (*Hint:* Use options on the Table Tools | Design tab.)

9 Format the table so that the header row is repeated on each page containing the table. (*Hint:* Use options on the Table Tools | Layout tab. You may need to first move the insertion point out of the table, then into the header row for this option to be available.)

10 Update and close the document.

Review questions

1 You have a table containing data that you want separated into two tables at a specific point. How can you do this?

2 Where can you find the setting for repeating the header row of a table?

3 You've applied a table style to a table, but the style formats the header row differently than the rest of the table. You want it formatted the same as the other rows. Where would you look to find settings to quickly adjust a table style?

4 You want to customize a table style beyond what is available in the Table Styles gallery. Where are the settings that you need to do this?

U n i t 3

Illustrations

Complete this unit, and you'll know how to:

A Use SmartArt to create and modify a diagram.

B Insert shapes in a document, and adjust their size, shape, and other attributes.

C Format text graphically using WordArt, drop caps, and text boxes.

Topic A: Creating diagrams

This topic covers the following Microsoft Office Specialist exam objectives for exam 77-418: Word 2013.

#	Objective
5.2	**Insert and format shapes and SmartArt**
5.2.2	Insert SmartArt
5.2.3	Modify SmartArt properties (color, size, shape)

Explanation

You can use Word to create diagrams, such as organization charts, that visually represent relationships or processes. To do so, insert a diagram by using the Choose a SmartArt Graphic dialog box, from which you can choose from some commonly used standard diagrams, such as process, cycle, or hierarchy diagrams.

SmartArt graphics

To insert a diagram into a document:

1 Place the insertion point where you want to insert the diagram.

2 On the Insert tab, click SmartArt to open the Choose a SmartArt Graphic dialog box, shown in Exhibit 3-1.

3 On the left, select a diagram type.

4 From the list of diagrams in that category, select the specific diagram you want.

5 Click OK to insert the diagram on a *drawing canvas* (the space in which you work on graphics or drawings). The Text pane appears, containing the diagram's placeholder text.

6 Click a text placeholder, and type the text you want to display in the diagram.

When you insert or work with SmartArt graphics, Word displays the SmartArt Tools | Design and SmartArt Tools | Format tabs.

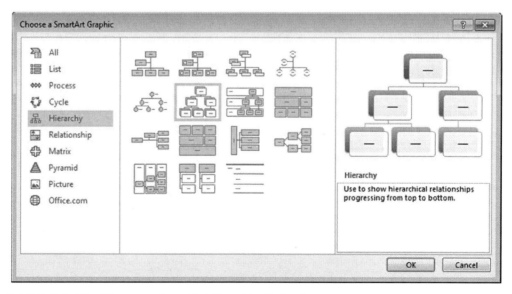

Exhibit 3-1: The Choose a SmartArt Graphic dialog box

Adding text to a SmartArt graphic

After your SmartArt graphic is inserted in a document, you can add text to it by using the Text pane. To show this pane, select the SmartArt graphic. Then, on the SmartArt Tools | Design tab, in the Create Graphic group, click Text Pane. (You can also click the control icon on the left edge of the frame that appears around the graphic when it's selected.) To hide this pane, click Text Pane again.

Do it!

A-1:   Creating an organization chart

Here's how	Here's why
1 Create a new, blank document	
Save the document as **My org chart1**	In the current topic folder.
2 On the Insert tab, click **SmartArt**	(In the Illustrations group.) To open the Choose a SmartArt Graphic dialog box.
On the left, select **Hierarchy**	
Click the indicated chart	The Hierarchy chart.
Click **OK**	To insert the organization chart on the page.
3 On the left edge of the chart, click the indicated area	(If necessary.) To display the text pane.
Under "Type your text here," click the first bullet	To select it so you can enter custom text.
Type **VP Global Sales**	The text appears in the top box of the chart.
4 Click the second bullet point	(In the Text pane.) This bullet is subordinate to the first, so the box is located in the second row of the chart, with a connecting line between the two boxes.
Type **Director North American Sales**	As you type, Word automatically aligns and sizes the text within the box.

5	Press ⏎ ENTER	To create another bullet point at the same level as the previous one. A new box is created on the second row.
	Type **Director Global Sales**	
6	Press ⏎ ENTER	
	Press TAB	To demote the bullet point to the third level.
	Type **Director European Sales**	

7	Press ⏎ ENTER and type **Director Pacific Rim Sales**	Type your text here
		
		• VP Global Sales
		  • Director North American Sales
		  • Director Global Sales
		    • Director European Sales
		    • Director Pacific Rim Sales
		
		To create another third-level bullet point. Now you'll remove the bullet points you don't need.

8	Place the insertion point in the [Text] bullet below the one you just added	
	Press DELETE	To remove the box from the chart.
	Press DELETE three times	To remove the remaining boxes. You can't delete the last box by pressing Delete.
	Press ← BACKSPACE three times	Each time you press Backspace, the box is promoted in the hierarchy; once it's at the top, pressing Backspace deletes the box.
9	On the Design tab, click **Text Pane**	(In the Create Graphic group.) To close the Text pane.
10	Update the document	

Formatting diagrams

Explanation

When you select a SmartArt diagram, a border appears around it, and Word adds the Design and Format tabs to the ribbon. You can use these tabs to change the layout and formatting of your diagram. Use the SmartArt Tools | Design tab to change the diagram type or layout, change the diagram shapes, and apply Quick Styles to the diagram. Use the SmartArt Tools | Format tab to modify and format individual diagram shapes and to format the diagram text.

Do it!

A-2:   Formatting an organization chart

Here's how	Here's why
1 Select the organization chart	(If necessary.) A frame appears around the chart when it is selected.
2 On the Design tab, click **Change Colors**	(In the SmartArt Styles group.) To display a color gallery.
Under Colorful, select the first option	(Colorful - Accent Colors.) To apply the color scheme to the chart.
3 In the SmartArt Styles group, click the More button	To display the SmartArt Styles gallery.
Under 3-D, select Inset, as shown	
	To apply the 3-D Inset style to the chart. Next, you'll format individual objects.
4 Click the boundary of the indicated shape	
	To select the shape.
Press (CTRL) and click the shape containing "Director Global Sales"	To select both shapes.
5 On the Format tab, click **Shape Fill**	(In the Shape Styles group.) To open the Shape Fill gallery.
Select the light blue color	Blue, Accent 1, Lighter 80%.
6 Update and close the document	

Topic B: Working with shapes

This topic covers the following Microsoft Office Specialist exam objectives for exam 77-418: Word 2013.

#	Objective
5.2	**Insert and format shapes and SmartArt**
5.2.1	Insert simple shapes
5.2.4	Wrap text around shapes
5.2.5	Position shapes

Explanation

You can add a variety of shapes to a Word document. You can add basic geometric shapes and symbols, lines, block arrows, flowchart symbols, callouts, stars, and banners.

Drawing shapes

You can draw shapes by selecting a shape from the Shapes gallery. To open the Shapes gallery, on the Insert tab, click Shapes. After selecting a shape, drag to draw it in the document. If you press Shift while drawing a shape, it will maintain its original proportions.

When you create or work with shapes, Word displays the Drawing Tools | Format tab on the ribbon.

Do it!

B-1:   Drawing a shape

The files for this activity are in Student Data folder **Unit 3\Topic B**.

Here's how	Here's why
1 Open Org chart2	
Save the document as **My org chart2**	In the current topic folder.
2 Click the chart	To select it.
3 On the Insert tab, click **Shapes**	To open the Shapes gallery.
Under Block Arrows, select the first arrow, as shown	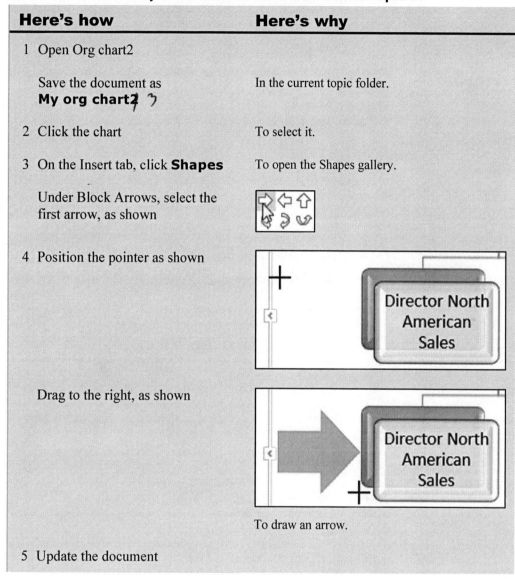
4 Position the pointer as shown	
Drag to the right, as shown	
	To draw an arrow.
5 Update the document	

Modifying shapes

After creating a shape, you can modify it in a variety of ways. You can move, resize, reshape, or rotate it. In addition, you can specify a shape's fill and outline.

Moving a shape

When you point inside a shape or along its edge, the pointer appears with a four-headed arrow at its tip, as shown in Exhibit 3-2. This pointer indicates that you can drag to move the shape. In addition, after you select a shape, you can press the arrow keys to nudge the shape in small increments for precise positioning.

Resizing a shape

When you select a shape, *sizing handles* appear at each corner and along each edge of the shape's boundary. When you point to a sizing handle, the pointer appears as a two-headed arrow, as shown in Exhibit 3-2. Dragging a sizing handle resizes the shape:

- Drag a sizing handle along an edge to change only the height or only the width.
- Drag a corner sizing handle to change the width and height.
- Press Shift while dragging a corner sizing handle to change the width and height proportionally.

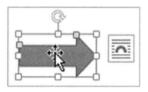 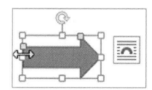

Exhibit 3-2: The pointer as it appears when placed within a shape (left) and when placed on a sizing handle (right)

Rotating a shape

When you select a shape, a rotate handle appears above it. When you point to the rotate handle, the pointer appears as a circular arrow, as shown in Exhibit 3-3. You can drag the rotate handle to rotate the shape.

Reshaping a shape

When you select a shape, it might display a yellow *adjustment handle*. You can drag an adjustment handle to reshape the shape. For example, with an arrow shape, you can change the thickness and length of the line part, change the size or shape of the arrowhead, or make the whole arrow short and thick or long and thin—to name just a few variations. When you point to an adjustment handle, the pointer appears as a white arrowhead, as shown in Exhibit 3-3.

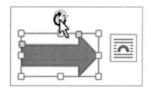 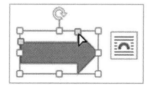

Exhibit 3-3: The pointer as it appears when placed on a rotate handle (left) and when placed on an adjustment handle (right)

Adding text to a shape

To enter text within a shape, right-click inside the shape and choose Add Text. Then type the desired text.

Arranging objects

The order in which objects overlap is known as the *stacking order*. Newer shapes or text boxes you create will appear in front of older items if they overlap. To change the stacking order, select an object and then select an option from the Arrange group on the Drawing Tools | Format tab. You can click the Bring Forward or Send Backward buttons, or you can click either button's arrow to display a menu with additional options for adjusting the stacking order.

To align shapes or text boxes with one another, first select all of the objects you want to align. Then, on the Drawing Tools | Format tab, click Position and choose the type of alignment you want.

Text-wrap options

You can change how text wraps around a shape by using the options in the Wrap Text menu on the Drawing Tools | Format tab. In addition, when you select a shape, the Layout Options icon appears at its top-right corner. You can click it to access the Wrap Text options.

You can control a shape's positioning and text wrapping with greater precision by using the Layout dialog box. For example, you can specify the text-wrap distance.

To specify text-wrap distance values for a selected shape:

1   On the Drawing Tools | Format tab, click Wrap Text and choose More Layout Options to open the Layout dialog box.
2   If necessary, click the Text Wrapping tab.
3   Select a Wrapping style.
4   Under "Distance from text," specify the minimum distance between text and each side of the shape.
5   Click OK.

Changing shapes into different shapes

After creating a shape or text box, you can convert it to a different shape. If you were to delete the current shape and start over, you'd have to draw the new shape and reapply all the formatting you applied to the old shape. However, if you simply change the current shape, it will retain any formatting you've already applied.

To change one shape into another:

1   Select the shape.
2   On the Drawing Tools | Format tab, click the Edit Shape button and point to Change Shape.
3   Select the desired shape.

Do it! **B-2: Modifying a shape**

Here's how	Here's why
1 Point to the arrow shape	A four-headed arrow appears at the tip of the pointer, indicating that you can click to select the arrow shape or drag to move it.
Drag the arrow to position it as shown	
2 Point to the left-center sizing handle, as shown	
	The pointer appears as a two-headed horizontal arrow, indicating that you can drag to change the shape's width.
Drag to the left	To lengthen the arrow shape.
3 Right-click inside the shape and choose **Add Text**	
Type **New position**	
4 On the Format tab, click **Edit Shape** and point to Change Shape	
Under Block Arrows, select the indicated shape	
	To change the arrow to a pentagon.
5 Update and close the document	

Topic C: Formatting text graphically

This topic covers the following Microsoft Office Specialist exam objectives for exam 77-418: Word 2013.

#	Objective
2.2	**Format text and paragraphs**
2.2.10	Change text to WordArt
5.1	**Insert and format Building Blocks**
5.1.2	Insert textboxes

This topic covers the following Microsoft Office Specialist exam objectives for exam 77-419: Word Expert 2013.

#	Objective
2.1	**Apply advanced formatting**
2.1.7	Link textboxes

Explanation

Word provides various ways you can apply graphical effects to text to add visual interest to a document. You can create WordArt objects, use drop caps, and add text boxes.

Working with WordArt

The "flag" of a newsletter (i.e., the newsletter's name) and the headline of a flyer are often stylized, as are other document elements that you might want to draw attention to. One way to stylize text is to use WordArt to create decorative effects from text. You can either create WordArt from existing text or insert a new text box.

To create WordArt from existing text in a document, first select the text. Then, on the Insert tab, click WordArt and select a style from the gallery, shown in Exhibit 3-4. (If no text is selected, Word creates the WordArt object with the placeholder "Your text here.") You can format the text as you would regular text in the document.

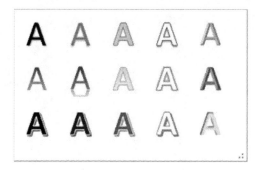

Exhibit 3-4: The WordArt gallery

When you select WordArt that has been inserted in a document, the Drawing Tools | Format tab appears on the ribbon. Using the tools on this tab, you can further modify the text, just as you would any other text in a document.

Do it!   ## C-1:   Using WordArt

The files for this activity are in Student Data folder **Unit 3\Topic C**.

Here's how	Here's why
1 Open Announcement	
Save the document as **My announcement**	In the current topic folder.
2 Select the first line of text	"A word from the chairman."
3 On the Insert tab, click **WordArt**	(In the Text group.) To open the WordArt gallery.
Select the indicated WordArt style	

(Fill - Blue, Accent 1, Shadow.) To create WordArt from the selection. Word creates a text box for the WordArt.

4 On the Format tab, click **Text Effects**	In the WordArt Styles group.
Point to **Reflection** and select the indicated option	

To ensure that the document text won't wrap around the sides of the WordArt.

5 At the top-right of the text box, click the Layout Options icon

Select the indicated option

6 Update the document

Using drop caps

Explanation   A *drop cap* is a large initial capital letter that extends below the first line of text in a paragraph. The drop cap adds visual interest and can be used to begin a document or a chapter, for example.

There are two variations of a drop cap: *dropped* and *in-margin*. Exhibit 3-5 shows a dropped drop cap; notice the way the text wraps around and below the dropped letter. Exhibit 3-6 shows an in-margin drop cap.

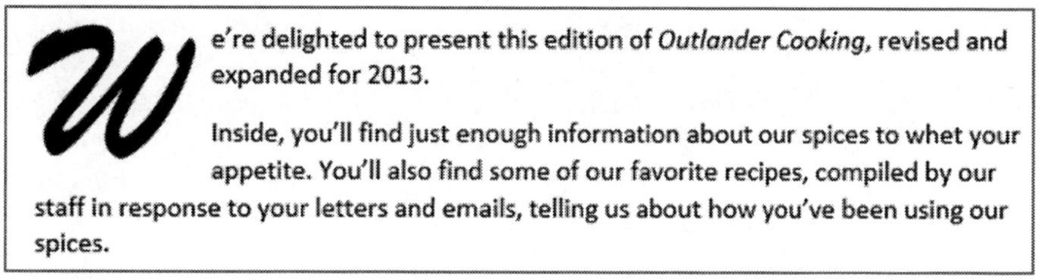

 e're delighted to present this edition of *Outlander Cooking*, revised and expanded for 2013.

Inside, you'll find just enough information about our spices to whet your appetite. You'll also find some of our favorite recipes, compiled by our staff in response to your letters and emails, telling us about how you've been using our spices.

Exhibit 3-5: A dropped drop cap

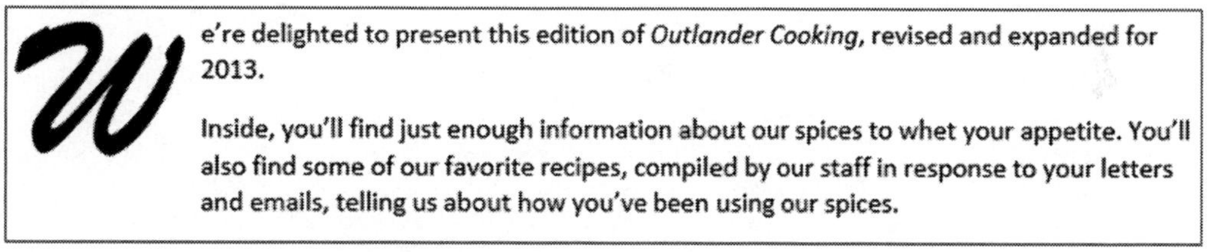

 e're delighted to present this edition of *Outlander Cooking*, revised and expanded for 2013.

Inside, you'll find just enough information about our spices to whet your appetite. You'll also find some of our favorite recipes, compiled by our staff in response to your letters and emails, telling us about how you've been using our spices.

Exhibit 3-6: An in-margin drop cap

To add a drop cap, place the insertion point in the paragraph that you want to begin with a drop cap. On the Insert tab, click Drop Cap and select the type of drop cap you want.

You can change the font of the drop-cap letter and change the distance of the text around it. To make these modifications, select the drop cap, click Drop Cap on the Insert tab, and choose Drop Cap Options to open the Drop Cap dialog box.

Do it! **C-2: Inserting and modifying a drop cap**

Here's how	Here's why
1 Place the insertion point in the first paragraph	It begins with "We're delighted to present."
2 On the Insert tab, click **Drop Cap**	In the Text group.
Point to **In margin**	To see a preview in the document.
Select **Dropped**	To create a drop cap. You'll modify its settings.
3 Click **Drop Cap** and choose **Drop Cap Options...**	To open the Drop Cap dialog box.
Observe the options	In addition to changing the position of the drop cap or removing it altogether, you can change its font and its distance from the text around it.
4 From the Font list, select **Brush Script MT**	To assign a different font to the drop cap.
Edit the Lines to drop box to read **4**	To increase the size of the capital letter to span four lines.
Edit the Distance from text box to read **0.1"**	To space the drop cap from the text slightly.
5 Click **OK**	To apply the changes.
6 Update the document	

Text boxes

Explanation

Text boxes are drawn objects in which you can enter text. You can arrange text boxes independently of other text or objects in the document area. To draw a text box:

1   On the Insert tab, click Text Box and choose Draw Text Box. The pointer changes to a large plus symbol.

2   Drag to specify the width and height of the text box.

3   Type to enter text in the text box.

Alternatively, you can insert a built-in text box by clicking Text Box and selecting one of the options from the gallery.

Formatting text boxes

You can format a text box, and you can format the text within a text box. To select and format the text in a text box, use the same techniques you'd use to select and format text in a typical document.

When you select a text box, the Drawing Tools | Format tab appears. Use the options on this tab to format the text box itself.

Linking text boxes

If you have two or more text boxes, you can link them to allow text to flow continuously from one text box to the next. To link two text boxes:

1   Enter the text in one text box, and keep that text box selected.

2   On the Drawing Tools | Format tab, click Create Link.

3   Click the empty text box where you want the text to be continued.

To break a link between text boxes, select any of the linked text boxes; then, on the Format tab, click Break Link. The link will be broken for each text box linked after the selected text box.

Pull quotes

A *pull quote* is a brief phrase excerpted from body text and typically enlarged or set apart from the body text by other formatting, as shown in Exhibit 3-7. You can use pull quotes to emphasize specific phrases or quotes and to add visual interest to a document.

In Word, you can insert a pull quote by using the Text Box gallery, or by drawing and formatting a text box.

*W*e're delighted to present this edition of *Outlander Cooking*, revised and expanded for 2013.

Inside, you'll find just enough information about our spices to whet your appetite. You'll also find some of our favorite recipes, compiled by our staff in response to your letters and emails, telling us about how you've been using our spices.

Also, be sure to check out our website, outlanderspices.com, for even more recipes, as well as for ordering information. All the spices used in this book are available for immediate ordering, and we stock many more. If you don't see it, ask, and we'll track it down for you.

We're sure you'll find enough here to keep you cooking for some time.

Exhibit 3-7: A pull quote

Do it!   **C-3:   Inserting a text box**

Here's how	Here's why
1 Select the fourth body paragraph	It begins "We're sure you'll find enough here." You'll place this text in a pull quote.
2 Press CTRL + C	To place the text on the clipboard.
3 On the Insert tab, click **Text Box**	(In the Text group.) To open the gallery.
Select **Austin Pull Quote**	To insert a text box with that style styled as a pull quote.
4 Press CTRL + V	To paste the text you copied earlier.
Press CTRL	To show the Paste Options.
Press T	To select the Keep Text Only option.
5 Drag the text box to the location shown	

We're delighted to present this edition of *Outlander Cooking*, revised and expanded for 2013.

Inside, you'll find just enough information about our spices to whet your appetite. You'll also find some of our favorite recipes, compiled by our staff in response to your letters and emails, telling us about how you've been using our spices.

We're sure you'll find enough here to keep you cooking for some time.

Also, be sure to check out our website, outlanderspices.com, for even more recipes, as well as for ordering information. All the spices used in this book are available for immediate ordering, and we stock many more. If you don't see it, ask, and we'll track it down for you.

6 Click the text box's Layout Options icon	
Select the indicated option	With Text Wrapping / Square
7 Update and close the document	

Unit summary: Illustrations

Topic A   In this topic, you used the **SmartArt** feature to create an organization chart, and you used the SmartArt Tools to modify the organization chart.

Topic B   In this topic, you created and modified a **shape**. You also converted a shape into a different shape.

Topic C   In this topic, you used **WordArt** and **drop caps** to format text graphically. You also inserted a **pull quote** in a document.

Independent practice activity

In this activity, you'll create and format a process chart. You'll also insert and format a text box.

1 Create a new, blank document, and save it as **My practice illustrations** in the Unit summary folder

2 Create a process chart that uses the Basic Process SmartArt graphic.

3 Name the diagram boxes **Meet supplier**, **Examine products**, and **Final approval**.

4 Add a fourth box on the same level with the text **Follow up**.

5 Apply the Colorful Range - Accent Colors 3 to 4 color scheme to the graphic.

6 Change the "Follow up" box shape fill to Orange, Accent 2.

7 Draw a text box above the "Examine products" box.

8 In the text box, enter **Test all products we plan to purchase**.

9 Format the text as Trebuchet MS, 10 pt, centered.

10 Change the text box to the Down Arrow Callout shape, shown in Exhibit 3-8.

11 Resize and reposition the text box as shown in Exhibit 3-9. (*Hint*: If necessary, specify a text wrap option.)

12 Update and close the document.

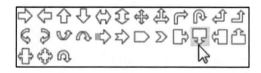

Exhibit 3-8: Selecting the new shape described in Step 10

Exhibit 3-9: The final text box shape as it appears after Step 11

Review questions

1 Which button on the Insert tab should you use to create a diagram?

   A Picture

   B SmartArt

   C Chart

   D Clip Art

2 How can you add text within a SmartArt diagram?

   A Draw a text box over the diagram box.

   B On the Insert tab, click Insert Object and choose Object.

   C Right-click the box and choose Insert Text.

   D Enter text in the Text pane.

3 Which ribbon tab should you use to change the color of a single box in a diagram?

   A SmartArt Tools | Format

   B SmartArt Tools | Design

   C Home

   D Page Layout

4 How can you create a shape that contains text? (Choose all that apply.)

   A On the Insert tab, click Text Box and choose Draw Text Box.

   B Draw a shape, click the Drawing Tools | Format tab, and click Text Wrapping.

   C Draw a shape, right-click it, and choose Add Text.

   D Draw a shape, click the Drawing Tools | Format tab, and click Shape Fill.

5 If a selected shape appears on top of another shape, where they overlap, how can you move the selected shape behind the other shape?

   A On the Drawing Tools | Format tab, click Change Shape.

   B On the Drawing Tools | Format tab, click Send Backward.

   C On the Drawing Tools | Format tab, click Align and choose Align Top.

   D On the Drawing Tools | Format tab, click Align and choose Align Bottom.

6 Where are the WordArt and Drop Cap tools located?

   A In the WordArt Styles group on the SmartArt Tools | Format tab

   B In the Design group on the Page Layout tab

   C In the Text group on the Insert tab

   D In the Styles group on the WordArt Tools | Format tab

Unit 4
Advanced document formatting

Complete this unit, and you'll know how to:

A Create and format sections of text by using section breaks, headers and footers, and page numbering.

B Format text into multiple columns.

C Customize a document's appearance by applying background colors, fill effects, watermarks, and themes.

Topic A: Creating and formatting sections

This topic covers the following Microsoft Office Specialist exam objectives for exam 77-418: Word 2013.

#	Objective
2.3	**Order and group text and paragraphs**
2.3.2	Insert breaks to create sections
2.3.4	Add titles to sections

This topic covers the following Microsoft Office Specialist exam objectives for exam 77-419: Word Expert 2013.

#	Objective
2.1	**Apply advanced formatting**
2.1.6	Create and break section links

Explanation

Some page layout settings, such as margins and page numbering, typically apply to an entire document. Sometimes, though, you might want to use different layouts in different parts of a document. You can do this by dividing the document into sections.

Section breaks

A *section* is a portion of a document in which you can set certain page layout options, such as margins, headers and footers, page numbering, and page orientation. By default, a document has only one section. However, you can create additional sections in a document—and even on a single page—and apply different settings to each one.

To divide a document into sections, you insert section breaks. These are inserted as hidden formatting symbols, so they're visible only if the Show/Hide button is selected or if you're viewing the document in Draft or Outline view.

To insert a section break, place the insertion point where you want to create a new section. Then, on the Page Layout tab, click Breaks to display the Breaks gallery, shown in Exhibit 4-1, and choose one of the four types of section break.

To delete a section break, place the insertion point just before it and press Delete.

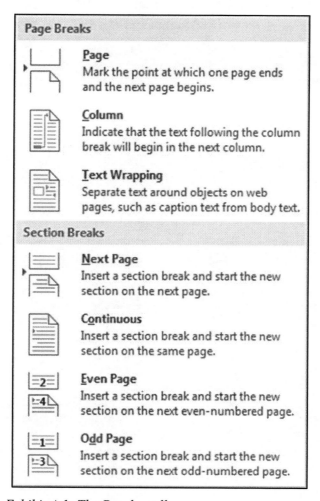

Exhibit 4-1: The Breaks gallery

Do it!

A-1: Inserting and deleting section breaks

The files for this activity are in Student Data folder **Unit 4\Topic A**.

Here's how	Here's why
1 Open Cookbook4	
Save the document as **My cookbook4**	In the current topic folder.
2 Scroll through the document	It begins with a letter, followed by a table of contents, a history of spices, spice descriptions, and recipes. Each portion is separated with page breaks. You'll insert section breaks.
3 Show the hidden formatting symbols	(Click the Show/Hide button.) To see the manual page breaks.
4 At the bottom of page 1, select the page break	(Click it.) This is where you'll insert the first section break.
Press (DELETE) twice	To delete the page break and the extra paragraph space. The insertion point is now at the beginning of the heading "Contents."
5 On the Page Layout tab, click **Breaks**	(In the Page Setup group.) To display a gallery with options for page and section breaks.
Under Section Breaks, choose **Next Page**	To create a section that starts on the next page.
6 At the bottom of page 2, delete the page break and the extra paragraph space	Click the page break to select it, and press Delete twice.
7 On the Page Layout tab, click **Breaks** and choose **Next Page**	There is a page break at the bottom of page 3. You'll leave it there because pages 3 and 4 are part of the same section.
8 At the bottom of page 4, delete the page break and the extra paragraph space	
Insert a Next Page section break before Bay leaf	
9 Create a section that starts on page 14	(The "Spicy Buzzard Wings" page.) Delete the page break on page 13, and insert a Next Page section break before the heading.
10 Hide the hidden formatting symbols	
Update the document	

Section formatting

Explanation

You can apply different page layout settings to different sections. For example, you can change the orientation and apply different margins and borders to each section. To change the page layout for a section, first make sure the insertion point is in that section.

To change the page layout for an entire document that contains sections:

1 Open the Page Setup dialog box.
2 From the Apply to list, select Whole document.
3 Specify the desired settings and click OK.

Do it!

A-2: Formatting sections

Here's how	Here's why
1 Press CTRL + HOME	To go to page 1, the first section in the document. You'll set margins for only this section.
2 On the Page Layout tab, display the Margins gallery and select **Wide**	To change the left and right margins to 2 inches.
3 Scroll in the document	Notice that Word has applied the new margin settings to only the first section.
4 Place the insertion point in the first section	If necessary.
5 Click **Margins** and choose **Custom Margins...**	(On the Page Layout tab.) To open the Page Setup dialog box with the Margins tab active. You'll specify custom margins.
6 Edit the Top box to read **2**	
Edit the Left box to read **1.25**	
Edit the Right box to read **1.25**	
In the Apply to list, verify that **This section** is selected	These changes will be applied to only the current section.
7 Click **OK**	To apply the margin settings.
8 Update the document	

Section headers and footers

Explanation

When you insert a header or footer in a section, that header or footer is applied by default to the entire document (assuming the default settings in the Options group on the Header & Footer Tools | Design tab—i.e. only Show Document Text checked). For example, if you insert a header in the third section of a document with five sections, that header will appear in all five sections.

To format the headers and footers differently for different sections, you have to remove the links between sections. To do so, activate the Header & Footer Tools | Design tab by editing either the header or the footer; then, in the Navigation group, click Link to Previous. Doing so removes the link between the current header or footer and the ones in previous sections. However, subsequent headers and footers (if any exist) will still be linked to the current one.

In addition, you can specify header and footer settings in the Options group that affect documents with sections. For example, checking Different Odd & Even Pages will specify that a header or footer appear only on the first page of a section.

While headers and footers are linked, any text you type in one header or footer will appear in all headers or footers. After they are unlinked, you can edit and format them independently. However, any text you've already entered and any formatting you've already applied will remain in the other headers and footers until you change them.

To tell whether a section header or footer is linked, check the bottom-right corner of the header or footer area, as shown in Exhibit 4-2.

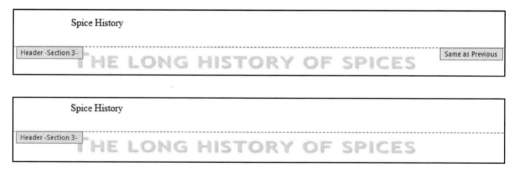

Exhibit 4-2: A linked header (top) and an unlinked header (bottom)

Do it!

A-3:   Inserting section headers and footers

Here's how	Here's why
1 Go to page 3	The third section of the document begins with the heading "The long history of spices."
2 Double-click the header area	(To edit it.) It's labeled "Header -Section 3-."
Type **Spice history**	
Observe the right side of the header	Same as Previous It indicates that this section's header is linked to the header of the previous section. You'll remove the link so that you can edit each section's header separately.
3 On the Design tab, click **Link to Previous**	(In the Navigation group.) To remove the link between the Section 3 header and the previous section header.
4 Click **Previous**	To go to the previous section header, on page 2. Because you entered text in the header before you removed the link, that text appears in every header in the document.
Delete the contents of the header on page 2	
5 Click **Previous**	To go to the header on page 1. Because the Section 1 and 2 headers are linked, when you deleted the text from the Section 2 header, the text in the Section 1 header was also deleted.
6 Click **Next** three times	To go to the header on page 6, the fourth section of the document. This section's header is linked to the previous section's header, so the text you entered there appears here as well.
Remove the link to the previous section's header	In the Navigation group, click Link to Previous.
Edit the header text to read **Spice descriptions**	
7 Click **Next**	To go to the header on page 15, the next section in the document.
Remove the link to the previous section's header	
Edit the header text to read **Recipes**	
8 Update the document	

Section page numbers

Explanation

Whenever you use the Page Number command to insert page numbers, Word automatically inserts page numbers starting at 1 and continuing consecutively through a document. For some documents, however, you might need more complex numbering. For example, many books contain introductory material that is numbered with Roman numerals—"page 1" doesn't actually begin until several physical pages into the book.

You can tell Word how to format page numbers for different sections by using the Page Number Format dialog box, shown in Exhibit 4-3. Word can number linked sections consecutively but format them independently. For example, if you insert a page number in the first section—and that section is linked to the second section—then the page number will appear in the first and second sections. However, if you use the Page Number Format dialog box to change the number format for the first section, the formatting will apply to only the first section, and not the second. Likewise, if you insert page numbers in subsequent, unlinked sections, Word will continue numbering pages consecutively unless you specify otherwise in the Page Number Format dialog box.

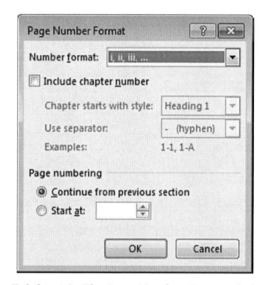

Exhibit 4-3: The Page Number Format dialog box

Do it!

A-4: Formatting section page numbers

Here's how	Here's why
1 Move to the Section 1 header	You'll format this page and the contents page to use lowercase Roman numerals as page numbers.
2 On the Design tab, click **Page Number** and point to **Top of Page**	To display page number options.
Select **Plain Number 3**	To insert a page number on the right side of the header.

3 Click **Page Number** and choose **Format Page Numbers...**	To open the Page Number Format dialog box.
From the Number format list, select **i, ii, iii ...**	To use lowercase Roman numerals, commonly used to number introductory pages in books.
Click **OK**	To close the dialog box.
4 Move to the Section 2 header	
Observe the page number	Word inserted a page number here because this header is linked to the previous one. It's numbered consecutively, but the format didn't change because this is a separate section.
5 Click **Page Number** and choose **Format Page Numbers...**	
From the Number format list, select **i, ii, iii ...**	
Click **OK**	To format this section's page numbers as lowercase Roman numerals.
6 Move to the Section 3 header	You'll insert a page number and set it to use Arabic numerals.
Place the insertion point after Spice history	
Press (TAB) twice	You'll insert the page number at the right margin.
Click **Page Number**, choose **Current Position**, and select **Plain Number**	This page is numbered 3. You'll change the numbering to start with 1 on this page.
7 Open the Page Number Format dialog box	Click Page Number and choose Format Page Numbers.
Under Page numbering, select **Start at**	The value defaults to 1, but you could select any number.
Click **OK**	
8 In Sections 4 and 5, insert page numbers using the format **1, 2, 3, ...**	Section 4 begins on page 5, and Section 5 begins on page 14. When you insert the page numbers, the first page in Section 4 will be numbered as page 3, and the first page in Section 5 will be numbered as page 12.
9 Double-click in the document area	To close the header and footer areas.
Update and close the document	

Topic B: Working with columns

This topic covers the following Microsoft Office Specialist exam objectives for exam 77-418: Word 2013.

#	Objective
2.3	**Order and group text and paragraphs**
2.3.3	Create multiple columns within sections

Explanation

Newsletters, brochures, and reports often present content in columns. Using columns can save space by enabling you to present more information on a page, as shown in Exhibit 4-4. This can help reduce the page count of a long document.

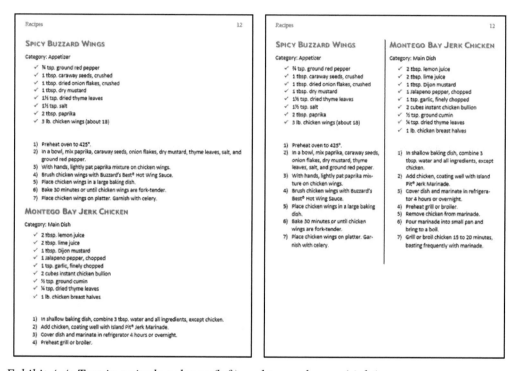

Exhibit 4-4: Text in a single column (left) and two columns (right)

Formatting text into columns

To format text into columns:

1 Select the text you want to format as columns. (Drag to select the text; or if you want to format an entire section, place the insertion point anywhere in that section.)

2 On the Page Layout tab, click Columns and choose More Columns to open the Columns dialog box, shown in Exhibit 4-5.

3 Under Presets, select a format. If you need more than three columns, enter the value in the Number of columns box.

4 Adjust the width and spacing of the columns as needed. (As you change the various settings in this dialog box, observe the Preview area to get an idea of how the selected text will look.)

5 Click OK.

You can also create columns by using the options in the Columns gallery.

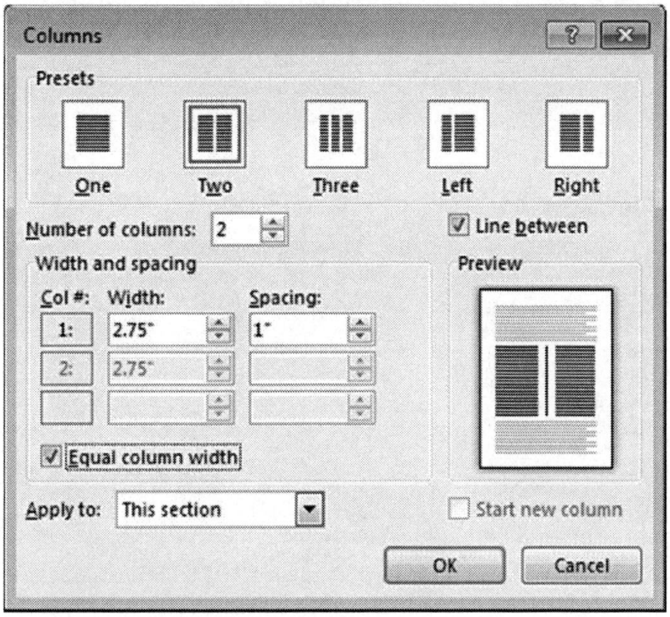

Exhibit 4-5: The Columns dialog box

Hyphenation

Often, when you format text into multiple columns, you'll find that the text doesn't seem to fit as well as when it's a single column. Word attempts to fit the text into the given space, but there might be large gaps between words (if the text is justified) or unusually ragged edges (if the text is left- or right-aligned). You can improve the appearance and readability of the text by turning on hyphenation.

To enable hyphenation, on the Page Layout tab; click Hyphenation and select Automatic. To specify more settings for how Word hyphenates, click Hyphenation and choose Hyphenation Options.

Adjusting the spacing between columns

You can adjust the spacing between columns to provide balance. For example, if the columns are too close together, the text might be difficult to read. To adjust the spacing:

1 Select the columns between which you want to adjust the spacing.
2 Open the Columns dialog box.
3 Under Width and spacing, in the Spacing box, enter the desired measurement (in inches). The Width box adjusts to accommodate the new spacing.
4 Click OK.

Column breaks

A *column break* is a mark that indicates the end of a column. When one of the columns is longer than another, you can insert a column break to balance them. The text after the break will move to the next column. You might also want to start a paragraph at the beginning of a column or move a heading to the next column to improve readability.

To insert a column break, place the insertion point where you want to insert the column break. Then, on the Page Layout tab, click Breaks and choose Column. To delete a column break, place the insertion point just before the break and press Delete.

Do it!

B-1: Formatting text into columns

The files for this activity are in Student Data folder **Unit 4\Topic B**.

Here's how	Here's why
1 Open Cookbook5	
Save the document as **My cookbook5**	In the current topic folder.
2 Place the insertion point in any of the recipes	In the last section of the document, beginning on page 14 (numbered as page 12).
3 On the Page Layout tab, click **Columns**	To display the Columns gallery.
Select **Two**	To have the text flow into two columns.
4 Scroll through the document	The column settings were applied to the last section only.
5 Click **Columns** and choose **More Columns...**	
Check **Line between**	To add a vertical line between the columns.
Edit the Spacing box for column 1 to read **0.25**	
	To set the space between the columns to 0.25".
Press (TAB)	The column width updates.
6 Click **OK**	
7 Click **Hyphenation** and choose **Automatic**	(In the Page Setup group.) Word applies hyphenation to the entire document. Some of the text re-flows.
8 On page 14, place the insertion point to the left of Montego Bay Jerk Chicken	The second recipe, in the left column. You want the recipe names to appear at the top of each column.
9 Click **Breaks** and select **Column**	To insert a column break. The text after the insertion point moves to the right column.
10 Insert a column break before Big D Veggie Chili	(On page 14.) Place the insertion point. Click Breaks and select Column.
11 Insert column breaks before the Crème Brûlée and Wasabi Pork Tenderloin recipes	
12 Update the document	

In the Spacing box illustration:

Col #:	Width:	Spacing:
1:	3"	0.25

Creating a heading that spans columns

Explanation

Even though you have text laid out in columns, you might want a heading that stretches across all of them, instead of across just one column. To add a heading that spans columns and uses the width of the page:

1 Place the insertion point where you want the heading to appear, and type the heading text.

2 Insert a Continuous section break after the text.

3 Place the insertion point in the section with the heading.

4 Set the number of columns to one.

Do it!

B-2:   Adding a heading across columns

Here's how	Here's why
1 On page 14, place the insertion point to the left of Spicy Buzzard Wings Type **Cooking with Outlander Spices**	
2 From the Breaks gallery, select **Continuous**	To create a section break that doesn't break across pages or columns.
3 Press (←)	To move the insertion point to the end of the heading you just typed.
4 Set the number of columns to 1	(In the Columns gallery, select One.) To make the heading span both columns.
Press (↵ ENTER) twice	To insert a blank line after the heading.
5 Place the insertion point in the line **Cooking with Outlander Spices** Center the text horizontally	
6 Update and close the document	

Topic C: Document design

This topic covers the following Microsoft Office Specialist exam objectives for exam 77-418: Word 2013.

#	Objective
1.3	**Format a document**
1.3.2	Change document themes
1.3.3	Change document style sets
1.3.5	Insert watermarks

This topic covers the following Microsoft Office Specialist exam objectives for exam 77-419: Word Expert 2013.

#	Objective
4.2	**Create custom style sets and templates**
4.2.1	Create custom color themes
4.2.2	Create custom font themes
4.2.4	Create and manage style sets
4.3	**Prepare a document for internalization and accessibility**
4.3.4	Manage multiple options for +Body and +Heading fonts

Explanation

You can customize the design of a document by using background colors and fill effects, borders, watermarks, or themes.

Background colors

To add a background color to a document, on the Design tab, click Page Color and select a color swatch. You can also apply special effects to the background. To do this:

1   On the Design tab, click Page Color and choose Fill Effects to open the Fill Effects dialog box, shown in Exhibit 4-6.

2   Use the Gradient, Texture, Pattern, and Picture tabs to specify the desired effects.

- Gradient – Apply multiple colors, which blend from one to another, as a background. Also used to apply various shading styles.

- Texture – Select the texture with which the color can be filled.

- Pattern – Select the pattern—such as dotted, line, or bars—in which the background color can appear.

- Picture – Apply a picture as the background.

3   Click OK.

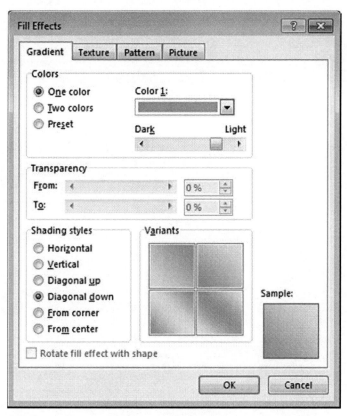

Exhibit 4-6: The Fill Effects dialog box

Page borders

To enhance the appearance of a document, you might want to add a border to one or more pages. To do so, on the Design tab and click Page Borders. In the Borders and Shading dialog box, select and customize the border. By default, page borders are applied to all pages in a document, but you can apply them to only specific sections.

Do it!

C-1:   Adding background colors, fill effects, and borders

The files for this activity are in Student Data folder **Unit 4\Topic C**.

Here's how	Here's why
1 Open Cookbook6 Save the document as **My cookbook6**	
2 On the Design tab, click **Page Color**	(In the Page Background group.) To display the Color gallery.
3 Select the indicated color	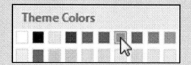 (Olive Green, Accent 3.) To apply the color as the document's background color. Next, you'll apply a gradient.
4 Click **Page Color** and choose **Fill Effects...**	To open the Fill Effects dialog box.
Under Colors, select **One color**	You'll combine the green background color with a lighter shade of the same color.
Drag the Dark/Light slider close to the right end of the bar, as shown	 To specify a lighter shade of the green color. If you drag all the way to the right, the green color will blend with white.
5 Under Shading styles, select **Diagonal down**	Four Diagonal down options appear below Variants.
Under Variants, select the top-right option, as shown	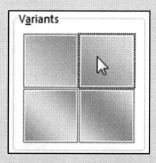
Click **OK**	To close the Fill Effects dialog box and apply the selected shading style.

6 Open the Fill Effects dialog box	In the Page Background group, click Page Color and choose Fill Effects.
Click the **Texture** tab	
Select the **Parchment** option, as shown	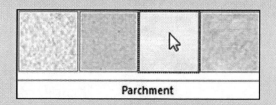
Click **OK**	To replace the previous background with a background texture that resembles parchment paper.
7 Click **Page Borders**	To open the Borders and Shading dialog box.
Under Setting, select the Shadow icon	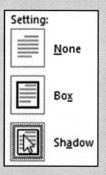
	In the Apply to list, Whole document is selected by default.
Click **OK**	To add the page border to the document.
8 Update the document	

Watermarks

A *watermark* is any text or image that can be seen behind the text in a document. For example, an organization's letterhead might have the company logo as a watermark. You can add text or a picture as a watermark.

You can select an option from the Watermark gallery on the Design tab. Or you can create a custom watermark. To do so:

1 On the Design tab, click Watermark and choose Custom Watermark to open the Printed Watermark dialog box.

2 Select Text watermark.

3 From the Text list, select the text you want to use as the watermark, or enter your own text in the Text box.

4 Format the text by using the Font, Size, and Color lists.

5 Click Apply to preview the watermark. Click Close.

To add a picture watermark, select the Picture watermark option in the Printed Watermark dialog box.

C-2: Adding a watermark

Here's how	Here's why
1 On the Design tab, click **Watermark** and choose **Custom Watermark...**	To open the Printed Watermark dialog box.
2 Select **Text watermark**	The text and font options are now available.
3 Edit the Text box to read **Outlander Spices DRAFT**	
Click **Apply**	To preview the watermark on the document page.
4 From the Font list, select **Arial Black**	(Scroll up in the list.) To change the font. You can also specify a size for the text, but here, you'll use the Auto default setting.
From the Size list, select **54**	
Click **Apply**	
5 Click **Close**	To close the dialog box. The watermark appears diagonally behind the page contents.
6 Scroll to view the document pages	To verify that the watermark appears on each page.
7 Update and close the document	

Themes

A *theme* is a named set of colors, fonts, and effects that can be applied to all pages in a document to provide a consistent look. When you apply a theme, the page formatting is changed, and the elements—such as background colors, heading styles, and table border colors—are customized based on the characteristics of the theme.

To apply a theme, on the Design tab, click Themes and select the desired theme from the gallery, shown in Exhibit 4-7. If you want to apply only the colors, fonts, paragraph spacing, or effects for a particular theme, you can select options from the appropriate lists in the Document Formatting group. *Theme effects* are graphical properties that are applied to any charts, SmartArt graphics, shapes, or pictures in a document. In addition, you can select an option from the Style Set gallery to specify font and paragraph properties for the entire document.

If you've specified a theme and have customized it by applying different colors, fonts, and effects, you can save the custom settings by clicking Themes and choosing Save Current Theme.

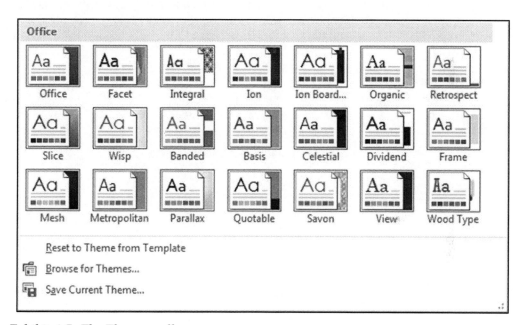

Exhibit 4-7: The Themes gallery

Theme fonts and default fonts

When you use a theme, Word specifies specific fonts for headings and body text. Those fonts are particular to each theme, and you can select different sets of heading and body fonts by choosing an option from the Fonts gallery on the Design tab.

To be more precise, themes apply the +Heading font to text that uses a heading style and the +Body font to all other text in the document (i.e., text that uses or that is based on the Normal style). You can think of these fonts as placeholders for the fonts specified by the theme (or selected from the Fonts gallery).

By default, the Normal template applies the +Body font to text in a document. However, you can specify a different default font, as well as default paragraph positioning and spacing. To do so, in the Styles task pane, click the Manage Styles icon; in the Manage Styles dialog box, click the Defaults tab. The settings you specify will become the new defaults for new documents based on the Normal template.

Restoring a template theme

If you change a document's theme, but later decide that you'd like to return to the original theme attributes, you can restore the original template theme. To do so, click Themes on the Design tab and choose Reset to Theme from Template.

Specifying a default theme

If you use a certain theme most of the time, consider making it your default theme. Then, when you create documents, that theme will automatically be applied.

To specify a default theme, first select a theme and specify any settings you want to use. Then, on the Design tab, click Set as Default.

Do it!

C-3: Applying themes

The files for this activity are in Student Data folder **Unit 4\Topic C**.

Here's how	Here's why
1 Open Cookbook flyer	
Save the document as **My cookbook flyer**	You'll use a theme to format this document. Currently, it uses the Office theme.
2 On the Design tab, click **Themes**	To display the Themes gallery.
Point to several different themes	Notice how the appearance of the document's fonts, colors, and SmartArt changes.
Select the **Retrospect** theme	You can change the characteristics of a theme.
3 Click **Colors**	(In the Document Formatting group.) To display a gallery of theme colors. You can select a set of colors from another theme, or customize the colors in the current theme.
Choose **Customize Colors...**	To open the Create New Theme Colors dialog box.
4 From the Text/Background - Light 1 list, select the indicated option	 (White, Text 1, Darker 15%.) To select a different color for all Text/Background - Light 1 document elements.
Click **Save**	To apply this change. It affects the background color of the SmartArt graphic.
5 Click **Fonts**	
Select **Century Gothic**	To modify the fonts used in the document.
6 Click **Effects**	To display a gallery of effects applied to any charts, SmartArt graphics, shapes, or pictures.
Select **Milk Glass**	To change the look of the SmartArt graphic.
7 Click **Themes** and choose **Save Current Theme...**	To open the Save Current theme dialog box.
Edit the File name box to read **My theme** and click **Save**	To save the custom theme.
8 Update the document	

Protecting document formatting

Explanation

After you've formatted a document, you might want to protect it so that you or others can't change it. To prevent someone from modifying or using styles or changing a document's theme, you can set formatting restrictions.

To prevent someone from changing a document's theme:

1 On the Review tab, click Protect Document to open the Restrict Editing task pane.

2 Under Formatting restrictions, click Settings to open the Formatting Restrictions dialog box.

3 Under Formatting, check Block Theme or Scheme switching, as shown in Exhibit 4-8.

4 Click OK.

Exhibit 4-8: The Formatting Restrictions dialog box

Do it!   **C-4:   Protecting a theme**

Here's how	Here's why
1 On the Review tab, click **Restrict Editing**	(In the Protect group.) To open the Restrict Editing task pane.
2 Under Formatting restrictions, click **Settings**	**1. Formatting restrictions** ☐ Limit formatting to a selection of styles Settings... **2. Editing restrictions** To open the Formatting Restrictions dialog box.
Check **Block Theme or Scheme switching**	
Click **OK**	
3 On the Design tab, observe the Themes button	It is grayed out, as are the Colors, Fonts, and Effects buttons. Themes and their components can no longer be changed in this document.
4 Open the Formatting Restrictions dialog box	In the Restrict Editing task pane, under Formatting restrictions, click Settings.
Clear **Block Theme or Scheme switching**	To remove the restriction.
Click **OK**	
5 Observe the Themes button	It is now available because you removed the restriction.
6 Close the Restrict Editing task pane	
7 Update and close the document	

Unit summary: Advanced document formatting

Topic A   In this topic, you learned how to insert and delete **section breaks**. Then you formatted pages in a section. Next, you inserted section **headers and footers**. You also formatted section page numbers.

Topic B   In this topic, you formatted text into **columns**. You learned how to insert column breaks, and you added a heading that spans multiple columns.

Topic C   In this topic, you learned how to apply **background** colors and **fill effects** to a document. You also created a **watermark**. In addition, you learned about **themes** and how they can be used to create a consistent look throughout a document.

Independent practice activity

In this activity, you'll create sections in a document. Then you'll insert page numbers and format text into columns. Finally, you'll apply a theme to the document.

The files for this activity are in Student Data folder **Unit 4\Unit summary**.

1 Open Newsletter1 and save it as **My newsletter1**. (*Note*: This document was created from a template.)

2 Create "next page" sections that begin on pages 2, 4, 5, and 6. (*Hint*: On page 6, insert the section break at the top of the page.)

3 In the header of each page, insert the page number by using the Accent Bar 2 style.

4 Unlink the header on page 6 from the previous header. Then delete the text in the header on page 6.

5 On pages 2 and 3, format the text into two columns.

6 Insert a column break so that page 2 appears as shown in Exhibit 4-9.

7 Format the heading and first paragraph on page 2 so that they span both columns. (*Hint:* After you insert the section break, an extra paragraph mark will appear in the first column; delete it.)

8 Apply the **Ion** theme to the document.

9 Change the page color to **Gold, Accent 3, Lighter 80%.**

10 Update and close the document.

Spices of the Month

Each month, we'll highlight two or three spices. We'll include background information on each spice, along with practical tips for using these spices in your own cooking.

Bay Leaves

Bay leaves come in many varieties. The popular American variety, also known as sweet bay and laurel, is a kitchen staple used widely to flavor meats, soups, stews, gravies, and vegetable dishes. The elliptical leaves are green, glossy, and generally grow to about 3 inches in length.

One of the most flavorful uses for Bay leaves is in the classic herb combination Bouquet Garni, with parsley and thyme. Traditionally, these fresh herbs are tied together, added to a dish, allowed to simmer, and then lifted out at the end of cooking. Dried herbs can be substituted and tied in a bit of cheesecloth. Add other herbs as the nature of the dish and your whims dictate. Try adding lemon, sage, and tarragon with chicken; rosemary and mint with lamb; green peppercorns, orange, and savory to beef.

Cilantro/Coriander

What many people don't realize is that cilantro is actually the leaf of the young coriander plant. Coriander is an herb in the parsley family, similar to anise. It is typically grown in California, although its origins trace back to the southern Mediterranean.

Chinese, Thai, and Indonesian cuisines are well known for their use of both cilantro and coriander. Chopped, the leaves, and the more pungent roots, add zest to most Thai curries, and the ground coriander seeds also give depth to the flavors. India curry powders owe a lot of their aromatic, citrus quality to ground coriander.

Before it is used, cilantro should be crushed, either by hand or with a mortar and pestle. Cilantro's taste is a fragrant mix of parsley and citrus. When cooking with cilantro, add it at the very end, as overcooking can muddy the taste.

Exhibit 4-9: Page 2 as it appears after Step 6

Spices of the Month

Each month, we'll highlight two or three spices. We'll include background information on each spice, along with practical tips for using these spices in your own cooking.

Bay Leaves

Bay leaves come in many varieties. The popular American variety, also known as sweet bay and laurel, is a kitchen staple used widely to flavor meats, soups, stews, gravies, and vegetable dishes. The elliptical leaves are green, glossy, and generally grow to about 3 inches in length.

Cilantro/Coriander

What many people don't realize is that cilantro is actually the leaf of the young coriander plant. Coriander is an herb in the parsley family, similar to anise. It is typically grown in California, although its origins trace back to the southern Mediterranean.

Exhibit 4-10: Page 2 as it appears after Step 7

Review questions

1 Why might you want to create sections?

2 Your document is divided into five sections, and you want to create a header in the third section. By default, any text that you enter is applied to the headers in which of the following?

   A Any sections that come after the current section

   B Any sections that come before the current section

   C Only the current section

   D Every section in the document

3 How do you change the spacing between columns?

4 How do you position a heading so that it spans columns?

5 How can you apply a solid background color to a document?

6 How can you apply a gradient background to a document?

7 On which ribbon tab will you find the Watermarks button for adding a watermark?

   A Home

   B Insert

   C Design

   D References

8 Which of the following will not be changed when you apply a theme to a document?

   A Colors

   B Page breaks

   C Fonts

   D Effects

Unit 5

Document sharing

Complete this unit, and you'll know how to:

A Use the Restrict Editing pane to protect a document with a password, and view and edit document properties.

B Track changes while editing, review and accept revisions, view changes made by different reviewers, restrict edits to tracked changes, merge revisions, and work with comments.

C Use the Compatibility Checker, the Accessibility Checker, and the Document Inspector to share documents.

Topic A: Document properties

This topic covers the following Microsoft Office Specialist exam objectives for exam 77-418: Word 2013.

#	Objective
1.4	**Customize options and views for documents**
1.4.6	Add values to document properties
1.5	**Configure documents to print or save**
1.5.5	Protect documents with passwords

This topic covers the following Microsoft Office Specialist exam objectives for exam 77-419: Word Expert 2013.

#	Objective
1.2	**Prepare documents for review**
1.2.3	Restrict editing
1.2.7	Protect a document with a password

Explanation

After you've created a document, you might want to protect it so that other users can't change something without authorization. You can assign a password to the document to protect it, and you can specify which kinds of changes you will allow people to make. In addition, you can view and edit document properties, which provide more information and can provide added security.

Protecting documents

You can protect documents by setting editing and formatting restrictions and by assigning passwords to them. Two types of restrictions can be assigned:

- *Formatting restrictions* prevent someone from modifying or using styles that you specify. This can effectively prevent other people from applying any formatting to a document.
- *Editing restrictions* let you select the kind of editing allowed in a document: Tracked Changes, Comments, Filling in forms, or No changes (Read only).

To specify formatting and editing restrictions:

1 On the Review tab, click Restrict Editing to open the Restrict Editing pane, shown in Exhibit 5-1.
2 Under Formatting restrictions, check the box to limit formatting to a selection of styles. Then click Settings to open the Formatting Restrictions dialog box. Select the desired options and click OK.
3 Under Editing restrictions, check the box to apply editing restrictions; then select an option from the list.
4 Under Start Enforcement, click "Yes, Start Enforcing Protection" to open the Start Enforcing Protection dialog box.
5 Enter a password; then reenter it to confirm it.
6 Click OK.

After a document is protected, you can remove protection by clicking Stop Protection in the Restrict Editing pane. When you do, the Unprotect Document dialog box opens, and you can enter the password.

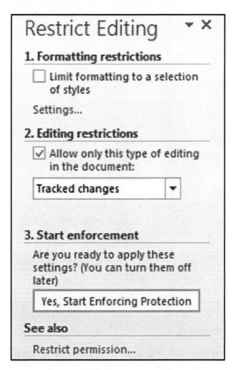

Exhibit 5-1: The Restrict Editing pane

You can also protect a document with a password without specifying formatting and editing restrictions. To do so, on the File tab, on the Info page, click Protect Document and choose Encrypt with Password. In the Encrypt Document dialog box, enter the desired password and click OK. When you're prompted to re-enter the password, do so and click OK again.

Once a document is password-protected, it can be opened only by entering the password. To remove password protection, click Protect Document on the Info page and choose Encrypt with Password. In the Encrypt Document dialog box, clear the Password box and click OK.

Password guidelines

When creating passwords, follow these guidelines:
- Passwords are case sensitive.
- Passwords can contain up to 15 characters.
- Any combination of letters, numerals, spaces, and symbols can be used.
- Including capital letters and numbers creates stronger passwords.
- Be sure to remember the password. Lost passwords cannot be recovered.

     ### A-1:   Protecting a document

The files for this activity are in Student Data folder **Unit 5\Topic A**.

Here's how	Here's why
1 Open Cookbook7	
Save the document as **My cookbook7**	In the current topic folder.
2 On the Review tab, click **Restrict Editing**	To open the Restrict Editing pane.
3 Under Editing restrictions, check the checkbox	
From the list, select **Tracked Changes**	
Under Start enforcement, click **Yes, Start Enforcing Protection**	To open the Start Enforcing Protection dialog box.
4 In the "Enter new password (optional)" box, type **password1**	
In the "Reenter password to confirm" box, type **password1**	
Click **OK**	To close the dialog box.
5 On page 1, change the heading from "A word from the chairman" to "Greetings from the chairman"	
Observe the document	The change you made is marked
6 In the Restrict Editing pane, click **Stop Protection**	(At the bottom of the pane.) To open the Unprotect Document dialog box.
In the Password box, type **password1** and click **OK**	You can now edit the document.
7 Close the Restrict Editing pane	
8 Update the document	

Within step 3, the illustration shows:

2. Editing restrictions
☑ Allow only this type of editing in the document:
[Tracked changes ▼]

Within step 5, the illustration shows:

Greetings| fro

Editing document properties

Explanation

Each Word document file stores information about the document itself. A document's properties are also referred to as *metadata*. To view and edit the properties of the active document, on the File tab, at the ride side of the Info page, click Properties and choose Show Document Panel.

The Document Panel, shown in Exhibit 5-2, appears above the current document. The panel provides a variety of information about the document. Enter information in the boxes to save that information as part of the document. You can then easily organize and identify your documents later based on this information.

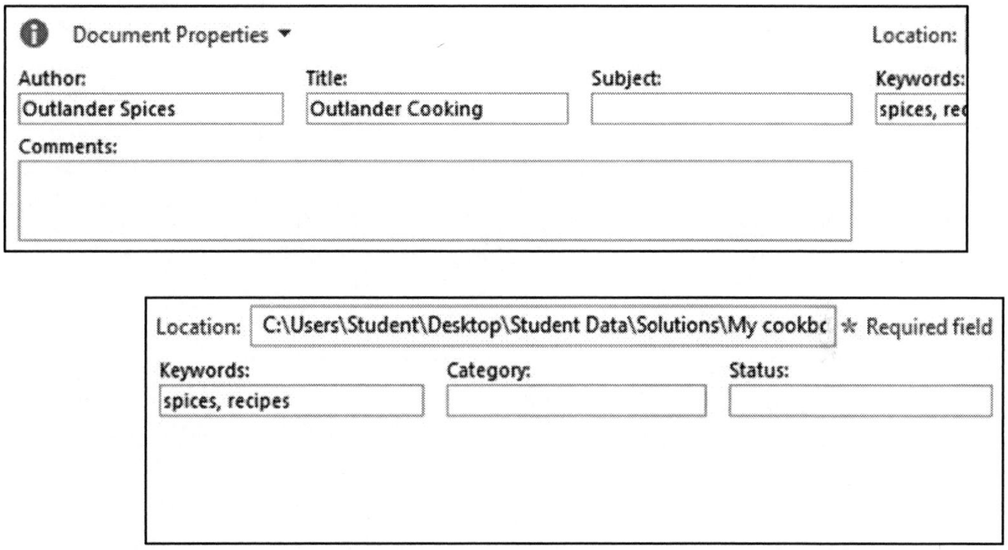

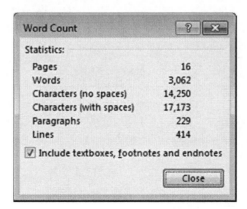

Exhibit 5-2: The Document Panel

Document statistics

To quickly display some statistics about a document, click the word count area on the left side of the status bar. This opens the Word Count dialog box, shown in Exhibit 5-3. The dialog box shows information about the text in the document.

Exhibit 5-3: The Word Count dialog box

To view even more statistics about the document, including the date it was created and modified, open the <Document> Properties dialog box. To do so, on the Info page of the File tab, click Properties and choose Advanced Properties.

A-2: Viewing and editing document properties

Here's how	Here's why
1 Click the **File** tab	To view the Info page, displaying information about the current document and its properties.
2 Under Properties, in the Title box, type **Outlander Cooking**	

Properties ˅	
Size	645KB
Pages	16
Words	3062
Total Editing Time	16 Minutes
Title	Outlander Cooking
Tags	Add a tag
Comments	Add comments

To add this metadata to the document.

3 In the Tags box, type **spices, recipes**	
4 Click **Properties** and choose **Show Document Panel**	To open the Document Panel above the current document. The properties you entered appear in the panel.
5 In the Document Panel, click as shown	

ⓘ Document Properties ˅

Author:

In the upper-left corner of the panel.

Choose **Advanced Properties...**	To open the Properties dialog box for the current document.
6 Click the **Statistics** tab	To display document statistics. You can see, for example, when a document was created, modified, and last accessed.
Click **OK**	To close the dialog box.
7 On the left side of the status bar, click the word count area	3062 WORDS

To open the Word Count dialog box, which displays some document properties.

Click **Close**	To close the dialog box.
8 Close the Document Panel	
9 Update and close the document	

Topic B: Tracking changes

This topic covers the following Microsoft Office Specialist exam objectives for exam 77-419: Word Expert 2013.

#	Objective
1.1	**Manage multiple documents**
1.1.2	Merge multiple documents
1.2	**Prepare documents for review**
1.2.1	Set tracking options
1.2.2	Limit authors
1.3	**Manage document changes**
1.3.1	Track changes
1.3.2	Manage comments
1.3.3	Demonstrate how to use markup options
1.3.5	Display all changes

Explanation

Your document might need to be reviewed by colleagues before it's finalized. If so, you can maintain a record of who makes which changes, and then you can choose to accept or reject each change. You can use the Track Changes feature to view changes and comments, and you can see changes made by specific reviewers.

Using Track Changes

To use Track Changes, either click the Track Changes button on the Review tab or press Ctrl+Shift+E. By default, changes are indicated by a vertical red line in the left margin. To modify the settings for Track Changes, on the Review tab, click the Tracking group Dialog Box Launcher to open the Track Changes Options dialog box; click Advanced Options to open the Advanced Track Changes Options dialog box, shown in Exhibit 5-4, in which you can customize how Word displays changes in the document.

By default, Word displays changes as Simple Markup. To specify a different display, select an option from the Display for Review list, shown in Exhibit 5-5. In addition, you can specify which markup appears by selecting an option from the Show Markup list.

For example, if you've used previous versions of Word, you might be accustomed to seeing revisions in "balloons" in the margin of the document, as shown in Exhibit 5-6. In Word 2013, only comments and formatting revisions are shown in balloons by default. To show all revisions in balloons, from the Show Markup list, choose Balloons, Show Revisions in Balloons; then, from the Display for Review list, select All Markup.

In addition, you might want to view only specific markup in a document. To do so, on the Review tab, click Show Markup and choose which elements to show or hide. By default, all of the options are selected.

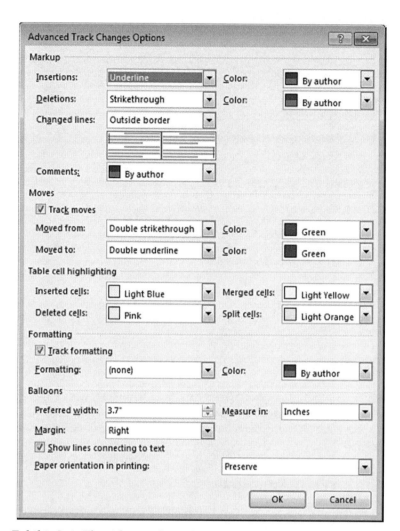

Exhibit 5-4: The Advanced Track Changes Options dialog box

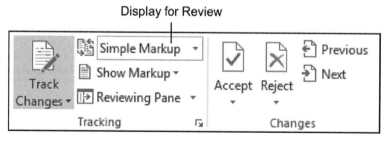

Exhibit 5-5: Track Changes options on the Review tab

Exhibit 5-6: Tracked changes and corresponding balloons in Print Layout view

Do it!

B-1: Tracking changes while editing

The files for this activity are in Student Data folder **Unit 5\Topic B**.

Here's how	Here's why
1 Open Cookbook8	
Save the document as **My cookbook8**	In the current topic folder.
2 Click the **Review** tab	
In the Tracking group, click the Dialog Box Launcher	To open the Track Changes Options dialog box.
3 Click **Advanced Options**	To open the Advanced Track Changes Options dialog box
Under Formatting, check **Track formatting**	To specify that Word indicates formatting changes. From the Formatting list, you could specify which formatting changes are tracked.
Click **OK**	To close the Advanced Track Changes Options dialog box.
Click **OK**	To close the Track Changes Options dialog box.
4 Click the Track Changes button	(In the Tracking group.) To enable change tracking. (If this feature is enabled, clicking the button again will disable it.)
5 At the end of the second body paragraph, type **In addition, we explore the long history of spices**, as shown	

> Inside, you'll find just enough information about our spices to whet your appetite. You'll also find some of our favorite recipes, compiled by our staff in response to your letters and emails, telling us about how you've been using our spices. In addition, we explore the long history of spices.
>
> Also, be sure to check out our website, outlanderspices.com, for even

The change is indicated by a vertical red line in the left margin.

6 In the first sentence of the second paragraph, select **just**

Type **more than**

> Inside, you'll find more than|enough

To replace the text.

7 Italicize the indicated paragraph

> *We're sure you'll find enough here to keep you cooking for some time!*

8 At the end of the letter, delete the Enjoy! paragraph

9 From the Display for Review list, select **All Markup**

(In the Tracking group.) To show markup inline with the text. The formatting change appears in a balloon in the right margin.

10 From the Show Markup list, choose **Balloons, Show Revisions in Balloons**

All revisions appear in balloons in the right margin.

11 Update the document

Reviewing revisions

Explanation

When someone else edits your work using Track Changes and returns it for your approval, you'll probably want to review the suggested changes. As you review the changes, you can either accept or reject them.

To accept or reject a change, select it and click either Accept or Reject on the Review tab. You can accept or reject all of the changes at once by clicking Accept and choosing Accept All Changes or by clicking Reject and choosing Reject All Changes. To quickly find changes, click Previous or Next.

Do it!

B-2:   Reviewing and accepting revisions

Here's how	Here's why
1 Place the insertion point at the beginning of the document	(Press Ctrl+Home.) You'll review the revisions.
2 On the Review tab, click **Next**	To select the first change in the document—"A word" was deleted.
In the Changes group, click the Accept button	To accept this change and move to the next one. The word "Greetings" was inserted.
Click the Accept button	To move to the next revision.
3 Click the Reject button twice	To reject the revisions—both the deletion and the insertion.
4 Click **Accept** and choose **Accept All Changes and Stop Tracking**	To accept the remaining revisions and deactivate Track Changes.
5 Update and close the document	

Multiple reviewers

Explanation

A document might be shared by several reviewers, who all make revisions to it. When viewing revisions, you can choose to view only the changes made by specific reviewers. To do so, on the Review tab, click Show Markup and point to Specific People to display a list with each reviewer's name, as shown in Exhibit 5-7. By default, All Reviewers is checked. To see only the changes made by a specific person, select the checked reviewers to hide their revisions; or first deselect all reviewers by choosing All Reviewers; then select the reviewer or reviewers whose revisions or comments you want to see.

To be identified by name as a reviewer, personalize your copy of Word. On the Review tab, click the Tracking group Dialog Box Launcher to open the Track Changes Options dialog box; then click Change User Name to open the Word Options dialog box. In the General section, type your name in the User name box.

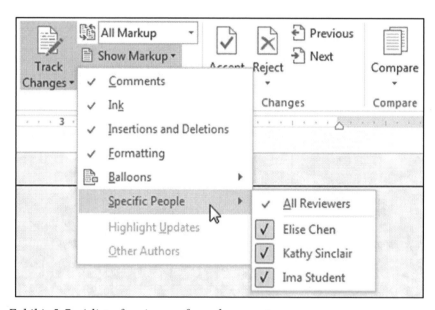

Exhibit 5-7: A list of reviewers for a document

Do it!

B-3:   Viewing changes by different reviewers

The files for this activity are in Student Data folder **Unit 5\Topic B**.

Here's how	Here's why
1 Open Cookbook9	
Save the document as **My cookbook9**	In the current topic folder.
2 Scroll in the document	To see the changes made by all of the reviewers. Each reviewer's changes are represented by a different color.
3 Click the Tracking group Dialog Box Launcher	(On the Review tab.) To open the Track Changes Options dialog box.
4 Click **Change User Name**	To open the Word Options dialog box.
In the User name box, type your name	
In the Initials box, type your initials	
Click **OK**	
5 Click **OK**	To close the Track Changes Options dialog box.
6 Enable Track Changes	Click the Track Changes button or press Ctrl+Shift+E.
On page 1, edit the heading as shown	

Greetings from <u>Outlander Spices</u>

7 Click **Show Markup** and choose **Specific People, Elise Chen**	To hide markups added by Elise Chen.
8 Click **Show Markup** and choose **Specific People, Kathy Sinclair**	To hide Kathy Sinclair's changes.
9 Click **Show Markup** and choose **Specific People, All Reviewers**	To show markups by all reviewers.
10 Update the document	

Comments

Explanation

While reviewing a document, you might want to insert comments. In Print Layout view, comments appear by default in balloons in the margin.

To insert comments in a document, either select the text that you want to comment on or place the insertion point where you want a comment to appear; then, on the Review tab, click New Comment and type.

To edit a comment you made, simply type in its comment balloon. You can also view and edit comments (and view other markup) in the Reviewing pane. To open it, click Reviewing Pane on the Review tab. To delete a comment, first place the insertion point either in the comment balloon or in the text to which the comment was added. Then, in the Comments group, click Delete and select an option.

In Word 2013, you can reply to comments, and they are shown in a single bubble, as shown in Exhibit 5-8.

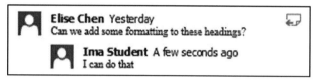

Exhibit 5-8: A comment thread

Do it!

B-4: Inserting comments

Here's how	Here's why
1 Click **Show Markup** and choose **Balloons, Show Only Comments and Formatting in Balloons**	
From the Display for Review list, select **Simple Markup**	To use Words default Track Changes settings.
2 Under the heading, select the first paragraph	It begins with "We're thrilled."
3 On the Review tab, click **New Comment**	A comment bubble appears to the right of the document.
Type **Doesn't really grab me**	
4 Move to page 5	(The heading is Bay leaf.) To view a comment made by a reviewer.
5 Point to the comment and click as shown	Elise Chen Yesterday Can we add some formatting to these headings? To reply to the comment.
Type **I can do that**	
6 Update and close the document	

Merging revisions into a new document

Explanation

There might be times when several copies of the same document have been circulating for reviewers to markup. Trying to manually combine all of the reviewers' marks into one document would be tedious. Instead, you can review the changes from two documents, decide which to keep, and then merge the two documents into a single document.

To merge two copies of a document in which changes have been tracked:

1　On the Review tab, click Compare and choose Combine to open the Combine Documents dialog box.

2　From the Original document list, select the first marked-up document.

3　From the Revised document list, select the second marked-up document.

4　Click More to display additional options in the dialog box.

5　Under Comparison settings, check all items that you want Word to compare.

6　Under Show changes in, select an option to identify which document the combined results should be shown in.

7　Click OK.

All tracked changes appear as marked revisions in the merged document, which appears in the Combined Document pane, shown in Exhibit 5-9. The two original documents appear in the Original Document and Revised Document panes. In addition, the Revisions pane provides a summary of all revisions in both documents. As in any other document, you can accept or reject each change.

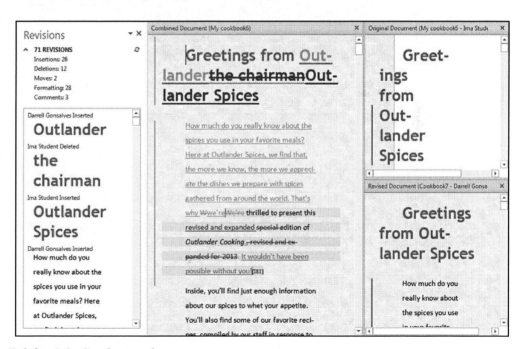

Exhibit 5-9: Combining documents

Do it!

B-5:   Merging revisions

The files for this activity are in Student Data folder **Unit 5\Topic B**.

Here's how	Here's why
1 On the Review tab, click **Compare** and choose **Combine...**	(To open the Combine Documents dialog box.) You'll merge two documents into one document that contains the changes from both.
2 From the Original document list, select **My cookbook9**	
From the Revised document list, select **Cookbook10**	These were originally the same document, but they now contain different changes.
3 Click **More**	To show more options for combining documents.
Under Show changes in, select **Original document**	To specify that the combined document show changes in to the document you selected as the Original.
Click **OK**	Several panes appear: Revisions, Combined Document, Original Document, and Revised Document.
4 Observe the Revisions pane	Revisions ∧ **71 REVISIONS** Insertions: 26 Deletions: 12 Moves: 2 Formatting: 28 Comments: 3 To see a summary of the revisions.
5 From the Display for Review list, select **All Markup**	To show all markup in the Combined Document pane.

6	Click **Next**	To select the first revision. Word highlights the word "Outlander" in the heading.
	Observe the Revisions pane	Darrell Gonsalves Inserted **Outlander**
		It indicates that Darrell Gonsalves inserted this word.
	Observe the Revised Document pane	It doesn't indicate that Darrell made this revision; apparently, a discrepancy is occurring between the two document versions.
	Click ☒	To reject the revision. Word highlights the next one.
7	Click ☑ twice	To accept both revisions you made earlier. Word highlights text that Darrell inserted.
8	Click **Accept** and choose **Accept All Changes and Stop Tracking**	
9	Observe the Revisions pane	It now indicates only the comments that are in the document.
10	Click **Delete** and choose **Delete All Comments in Document**	In the Comments group.
11	Update and close the document	To close all three document panes.
12	Close the Revisions pane	

Topic C: Finalizing documents

This topic covers the following Microsoft Office Specialist exam objectives for exam 77-419: Word Expert 2013.

#	Objective
1.2	**Prepare documents for review**
1.2.5	Remove document metadata
1.2.6	Mark as final
4.3	**Prepare a document for internalization and accessibility**
4.3.2	Add alt-text to document elements
4.3.3	Create documents for use with accessibility tools
4.3.6	Modify tab order in document elements and objects

Explanation

When a document is complete, you can use a series of features to finalize it before sharing it with others. On the File tab, the Info page contains options for protecting the document, checking for issues, and modifying properties.

The Document Inspector

The *Document Inspector* checks for hidden metadata, such as comments, and for personal information that you might not want other readers to see. To open the Document Inspector, click the File tab and click Info. On the Info page, click the Check for Issues button and choose Inspect Document. Click Inspect to start the evaluation. The results are displayed in the Document Inspector dialog box, shown in Exhibit 5-10.

The Document Inspector checks the following elements:

- Comments, revisions, and annotations
- Document properties and personal information
- Task pane apps
- Collapsed headings
- Custom XML data
- Headers, footers, and watermarks
- Invisible content
- Hidden text

If Word finds an issue, it is displayed in the Document Inspector dialog box. You're given the option to remove the content that's causing the issue. For example, if there's document metadata that you want to remove, in the Document Inspector dialog box, click Remove All.

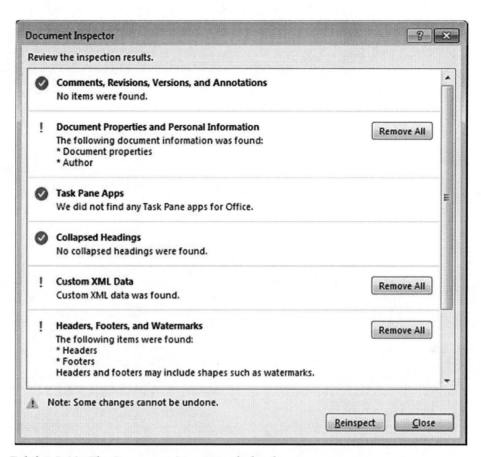

Exhibit 5-10: The Document Inspector dialog box

Finalizing a document

To finalize a document, display the Info page, click the Protect Document button, and choose Mark as Final. By marking a document as Final, you indicate that editing is completed, and the file is then read-only. Word disables typing, editing commands, and proofing marks. The status property is set to Final, and the Mark As Final icon is displayed in the status bar. (To make the document editable again, repeat the steps you used to mark it as final.)

Do it!

C-1: Inspecting and finalizing a document

The files for this activity are in Student Data folder **Unit 5\Topic C**.

Here's how	Here's why
1 Open Cookbook11	
Save the document as **My cookbook11**	In the current topic folder.
2 On the File tab, click **Check for Issues** and choose **Inspect Document**	(On the Info page.) To open the Document Inspector dialog box.
Observe the categories	You can clear any element that you don't want to include in the inspection.
3 Click **Inspect** and observe the results	The Document Inspector identifies document properties, custom XML data, and headers and footers as elements that you might want to remove before sharing this document.
For Document Properties and Personal Information, click **Remove All**	To remove the author name and document title. You don't want others to see the names of people who worked on the document.
4 Click **Close**	To return to the Info page.
5 Click **Protect Document** and choose **Mark as Final**	A message box appears, stating that this will mark the document as final and make it read-only.
Click **OK**	Another message box appears, explaining that because this file is now final, it can no longer be edited.
Click **OK**	
6 Press (ESC)	To return to the Home tab.
7 Observe the Information bar at the top of the document	

> ⓘ MARKED AS FINAL An author has marked this document as final to discourage editing. [Edit Anyway]

	It tells you that the file has been marked as final, to discourage editing, and gives you the option to edit it anyway.
Observe the icon on the left side of the status bar	(The Marked as Final icon.) This indicates that the document has been saved and finalized.

The Accessibility Checker

Explanation

For users with disabilities, viewing and reading electronic documents can be challenging. It's a good idea to check to see whether your document meets some basic accessibility standards before finalizing and distributing it, especially if you expect it to be viewed by many different users. People with disabilities will likely view a document by using screen reader software, which attempts to interpret and identify what is shown on the screen.

In Word, you can use the Accessibility Checker task pane to highlight potential accessibility issues. To do so, on the File tab, click Info; then click Check for Issues and select Check Accessibility. In the Accessibility Checker task pane, shown in Exhibit 5-11, you can click each item to go to it in the document. In addition, the task pane displays information about the issue when you select an item. The accessibility issues fall into three categories:

- **Error** – Content that would be very difficult or impossible for people with disabilities to understand.

- **Warning** – Content that can, in most cases, be difficult for people with disabilities to understand.

- **Tip** – Content that could be understood by people with disabilities but that might be better understood if organized or presented differently.

To meet the standards for accessibility, you should follow these guidelines when designing a document:

- **Add alternative text to images and objects.** "Alt text" provides descriptions of content such as pictures or tables. To add alt text to objects:
  - For pictures, charts, shapes, and other graphics, right-click the object and choose the Format option. In the task pane, click the Layout & Properties icon and enter information in the Alt Text section. (the Description box should always be completed; the Title box, which provides a brief description of the content, is optional.)
  - For tables, right-click the table and choose Table Properties. In the Table Properties dialog box, enter information on the Alt Text tab.

- **Specify column header rows in tables.** Column headings can assist navigation. To specify a column heading, select the desired row and, on the Table Tools | Design tab, check Header Row.

- **Use styles in long documents.** Styles, for both headings and paragraphs, provide a structure that can make it easier for a screen reader to interpret content in the appropriate order.

- **Use short headings.** Long headings (more than 20 words, or more than one line) can make it difficult for a screen reader to navigate a document.

- **Ensure heading styles are in the correct order.** Apply heading styles in a logical order. So, for example, Heading 2 should be a child of Heading 1. Likewise, apply outline levels to styles in the same way.

- **Use meaningful hyperlink text.** You can specify descriptive text that appears when a user points to a hyperlink. To do so, select the text you want to make a hyperlink and, on the Insert tab, click Hyperlink; in the "Text to display" box, enter a brief description of the link destination.

- **Use simple table structure.** Nested tables or tables that contain merged or split cells can be difficult to navigate. To test this, place the insertion point in the first cell and press Tab repeatedly to move through the table elements. Modify the table as necessary so that someone could move through the table logically by pressing Tab.

- **Avoid using blank cells for formatting.** Blank cells in a table might indicate to a screen reader that it has reached the end of the table, when in fact it hasn't. When possible, remove blank cells. Alternatively, you can clear formatting from a blank cell; to do so, on the Table Tools | Design tab, display the Table Styles gallery and choose Clear.

- **Avoid repeated blank characters.** Extra spaces, tab marks, or empty paragraphs might be interpreted by a screen reader as "blank," indicating to the user that there's no more content. Remove unnecessary white space and use paragraph formatting to create indents, rather than spaces or tabs.

- **Avoid floating objects.** When specifying text wrap, use the In Line with Text or Top and Bottom settings.

- **Avoid image watermarks.** Image watermarks can be misinterpreted. To make sure the content is understood, include the information elsewhere in the document as well.

- **Include closed captions for audio.** If you use audio elements, make sure that they include closed captions, transcripts, or alt text.

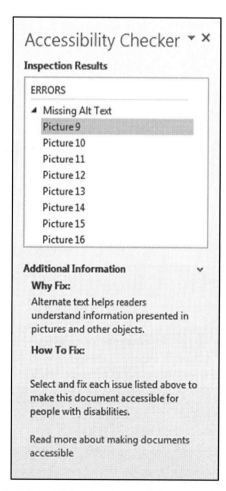

Exhibit 5-11: The Accessibility Checker task pane

Do it!

C-2: Checking accessibility

Here's how	Here's why
1 On the File tab, click **Check for Issues** and choose **Check Accessibility**	To open the Accessibility Checker task pane.
2 Under Missing Alt Text, click **Picture 9**	To go to the first picture that's missing alternative text.
In the information bar, click **Edit Anyway**	Since the file was marked as final, you will have to enable editing again to format the picture.
3 Right-click the bay leaves picture and choose **Format Picture...**	To open the Format Picture task pane.
Click	The Layout & Properties icon, in the Format Picture task pane.
4 Click **Alt Text**	
In the Title box, type **Bay leaf**	
In the Description box, type **Image of whole bay leaves**	
5 Observe the Accessibility Checker task pane	Picture 9 no longer appears in the list under Alt Text.
Observe the Warnings list	It lists pictures that aren't inline
6 Click the bay leaves image	(In the document.) If necessary.
Click the Layout Options button	On the Format tab.
Click	The In Line with Text icon.
Place the insertion point after the Bay Leaf heading and press (↵ ENTER)	To move the picture to the next paragraph.
7 Observe the Accessibility Checker task pane	Picture 9 no longer appears in the list under Objects not Inline.
8 Close the Accessibility Checker task pane	
Close the Format Picture task pane	
9 Update the document	

DBL

The Compatibility Checker

Explanation

If you're sharing your documents with others who use previous versions of Word, you'll want to check for elements that aren't supported or that behave differently in these other versions. These elements can include a number of things. To check for unsupported elements, use the Compatibility Checker.

To run the Compatibility Checker, display the Info page; click the Check for Issues button and choose Check Compatibility. From the Select versions to show drop-down list, select the versions you want to show: Word 97-2003, Word 2007, or Word 2010. All three options are selected by default.

Incompatibilities are identified and listed for your review. If you export a document to the Word 97-2003 file format, the Compatibility Checker will run automatically. To save a file in this format, on the File tab, click Export; then click Change File Type and select Word 97-2003 Document. Click Save As to save the document as a file with the .doc extension.

Do it!

C-3: Using the Compatibility Checker

The files for this activity are in Student Data folder **Unit 5\Topic C**.

Here's how	Here's why
1 On the File tab, click **Export**	
Click **Change File Type**	
Select **Word 97-2003 Document**	To save the file in the .doc file format.
2 Click **Save As** and navigate to the current topic folder	
Click **Save**	The Compatibility Checker runs automatically, opening the Microsoft Word Compatibility Checker dialog box.
3 Observe the message	To see a summary of what will change when the file is converted to the earlier format.

Some text box positioning will change.	1
	Help
Shapes and textboxes will be converted to effects available in this format.	1
Effects on text will be removed.	3

4 Click **Continue**	To accept this alteration and continue saving the document in the Word 97-2003 format.
5 Observe the title bar	Word is now operating in Compatibility mode.
6 Close the document	

Unit summary: Document sharing

Topic A   In this topic, you used the Restrict Editing pane to **protect** a document with a password. Then you viewed and edited document **properties**. You also learned how to display a document's statistics.

Topic B   In this topic, you learned how to enable Word's **Track Changes** feature and change its settings. You also learned how to review and accept revisions, and view changes made by different reviewers. Next, you inserted a **comment** and replied to a comment from another reviewer. In addition, you learned how to **merge revisions** from two documents into one.

Topic C   In this topic, you used the **Compatibility Checker** and the **Document Inspector** to prepare a document for sharing with others. You also learned about using the **Accessibility Checker** to identify problems your document might present for users with disabilities.

Independent practice activity

In this activity, you'll enable password protection for a document and edit its properties. Then you'll enable Track Changes to record the revisions you make in a document. Next, you'll compare your revisions with those of another reviewer and combine them into one document. Finally, you'll inspect and finalize the document.

The files for this activity are in Student Data folder **Unit 5\Unit summary**.

1 Open Herbs and spices1, and save it as **My herbs and spices1**.

2 Protect the document so that only tracked changes are allowed without the password **password**.

3 Show the document properties.

4 In the Author field, enter your name.

5 Close the Document Properties pane.

6 On page 2, edit the heading "Healing benefits of herbs" to read **Health benefits of herbs**.

7 Add this comment to the heading you edited: **Find sources for these claims?**

8 Disable document protection. Then update and close the document, and close the Restrict Editing pane.

9 Compare the revisions in the document My herbs and spices1 with those in the document Herbs and spices2. Specify that changes be shown in the original document (i.e., My herbs and spices1). (*Hint*: When Word asks whether you want to mark tracked changes as accepted, click Yes.)

10 Accept all changes in the combined document.

11 Delete all comments from the document.

12 Inspect the document and delete any personal information.

13 Mark the document as final.

14 Close the document, and close the Revisions pane.

Review questions

1 Where can you set a password to protect a document from unwanted edits?

   A The Restrict Editing pane

   B The Properties pane

   C The Application Settings dialog box

   D The Password group

2 How do you turn on the Track Changes feature?

3 You want to send your document out for review, and you want to ensure that all edits are recorded as tracked changes. What should you do?

4 If you want to verify that a document contains metadata that might reveal personal information, what tool can you use?

   A The Find command

   B The Compatibility Checker

   C The Restrict Editing pane

   D The Document Inspector

5 To check your document for issues that might present problems for users with disabilities, such as those relying on screen reader software, what tool would you use?

   A The Document Inspector

   B The Accessibility Checker

   C The Compatibility Checker

   D The Restrict Editing pane

Unit 6

Mail Merge

Complete this unit, and you'll know how to:

A Use the Mailings tab to create form letters.

B Create a recipient list, sort records, and filter records.

C Create mailing-label and envelope documents by using a recipient list.

Topic A: Form letters

This topic covers the following Microsoft Office Specialist exam objectives for exam 77-418: Word 2013.

#	Objective
5.1	**Insert and format Building Blocks**
5.1.1	Insert Quick Parts

This topic covers the following Microsoft Office Specialist exam objectives for exam 77-419: Word Expert 2013.

#	Objective
2.1	**Apply advanced formatting**
2.1.2	Create custom field formats
3.3	**Manage forms, fields, and Mail Merge operations**
3.3.1	Add custom fields
3.3.2	Modify field properties
3.3.5	Perform mail merges
3.3.6	Manage recipient lists
3.3.7	Insert merged fields
3.3.8	Preview results

Explanation

When you need to mail a form letter to multiple recipients, you can save time by using Word's Mail Merge feature to generate all of the letters from a single document. Most of the text in the letter will be identical for all recipients, but some specific elements—such as the recipient's name and address—will be different in each letter.

Inserting standard fields

Before you begin the mail merge process, you might want to insert several standard fields into your letter. A *field* is a placeholder for data that can change. For example, you can use a field to insert a date that is automatically updated.

To insert a field:

1. On the Insert tab, click Quick Parts and choose Field to open the Field dialog box, shown in Exhibit 6-1.
2. From the Categories list, select a category.
3. Under Field names, select the field you want to insert.
4. Under Field properties and Field options, specify any additional settings needed.
5. Click OK.

In the document, fields are shaded gray when they're selected. Each field has a *field code*, which is the underlying instruction that provides the necessary result.

Modifying fields

After inserting a field, you can modify it by right-clicking it and choosing Edit Field to open the Field dialog box. The options in the Field dialog box will reflect the type of field you right-clicked. Specify the changes you want and click OK.

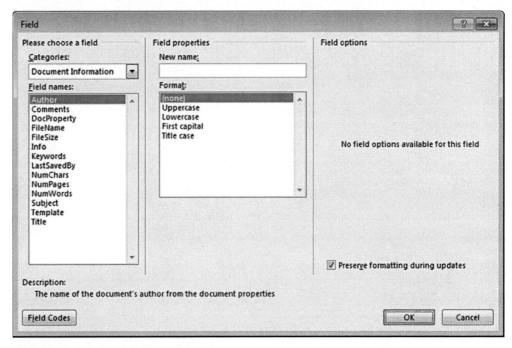

Exhibit 6-1: The Field dialog box

Custom fields

Besides the standard fields that you can insert, you can also create and insert custom fields. Instead of using information from the document, custom fields can contain any information you want. To create a custom field:

1   On the File tab, click Info.
2   Click Properties and select Advanced Properties.
3   Select a field name.
4   From the Type list, select the kind of content you want the field to contain.
5   In the Value box, enter the desired content.
6   Click Add.
7   When finished adding custom fields, click OK.

To insert a custom field, in the Field dialog box, under Field name, select DocProperty. Then, under Property, select the desired field and click OK.

Do it!

A-1:   Working with fields

The files for this activity are in Student Data folder **Unit 6\Topic A**.

Here's how	Here's why
1 Open Letter1	(From the current topic folder.) Before you begin the mail merge process, you'll insert and modify a few standard fields.
Save the document as **My letter1**	In the current topic folder.
2 Click the **File** tab	To display the document's standard properties. (The Info option is selected by default.)
3 Under Properties, right-click the **Author** icon and choose **Edit Property**	Author [Copy / Remove Person / Edit Property / Open Contact Card] Last Modified By
	To open the Edit person dialog box.
Press (ESC)	To close the search box.
In the box, type your name, then click **OK**	
4 Click **Properties** and select **Advanced Properties**	To open the My letter1 Properties dialog box.
Click the **Custom** tab	
5 Under Name, select **Department**	
In the Value box, enter **Media Relations**	
Click **Add**	To add the custom field.
Click **OK**	To close the dialog box.
6 Press (ESC)	To return to the letter.
7 At the bottom of the letter, select **Chris Carr**	You'll insert the Author field to replace the selected text with your own name.

8 On the Insert tab, click **Quick Parts** and choose **Field...**	(In the Text group.) To open the Field dialog box.
From the Categories list, select **Document Information**	To display the Document Information fields. Author is selected.
Click **OK**	To insert your name as the document author.
9 Press (↵ *ENTER*)	To create a blank paragraph.
On the Insert tab, click **Quick Parts** and choose **Field...**	
Under Field names, select **DocProperty**	
Under Property, select **Department**	The custom field you created.
Click **OK**	To insert the Department field.
10 At the top of the letter, right-click the date and choose **Edit Field...**	To open the Field dialog box.
Under Date formats, select the sample date that uses the format **MMMM d, yyyy**, as shown	MMMM d, yyyy 2/26/2013 Tuesday, February 26, 2013 February 26, 2013
Click **OK**	The date uses the new format.
11 Update the document	

Steps in a mail merge

Explanation

To create a form letter, use Word's Mail Merge feature. The mail merge options are located on the Mailings tab. The following are the basic steps for a mail merge:

1 Create a starting document, which can be a letter, email message, envelope, label, or directory.

2 Specify a list of recipients; this list should include the data that will change for each letter, such as name and address. You can create the data list in Word while you perform the mail merge, or you can use a list from another document or from your Outlook contacts.

3 Insert the data from the recipient list into the starting document. Each piece of data you insert is called a *merge field*. It appears as a placeholder representing data from the recipient list, as shown in Exhibit 6-2. The value in this field appears when you merge the starting document with the recipient list.

4 Merge the starting document with the recipient list. The merge fields are replaced with the data from the recipient list, as shown in Exhibit 6-3.

«AddressBlock»

«GreetingLine»

Because you are an important communicator in the food and restaurant industry in «City» and beyond, I invite you to take advantage of the enclosed press kit from Outlander Spices. Outlander Spices plays a unique and vital role in the food and restaurant industry, and I think you'll find that we provide information and perspectives you might not have encountered elsewhere.

Exhibit 6-2: A document containing merge fields

Janice Finnegan

Healthy Eating Magazine

102 S. Main Street

Astoria, OR 97223

To Janice Finnegan,

Because you are an important communicator in the food and restaurant industry in Astoria and beyond, I invite you to take advantage of the enclosed press kit from Outlander Spices. Outlander Spices plays a unique and vital role in the food and restaurant industry, and I think you'll find that we provide information and perspectives you might not have encountered elsewhere.

Exhibit 6-3: A document after merging with a recipient list

Identifying a starting document and recipients

If you have a document containing a list of recipients, such as a Word table, an Excel spreadsheet, an Outlook table, or an Access table, you can specify that document as your recipient list. To specify a starting document and a recipient list document for a form letter:

1 Open or create the starting document that contains the letter text.

2 On the Mailings tab, click Start Mail Merge. From the menu that appears, choose Letters, as shown in Exhibit 6-4, to specify that the starting document is a letter.

3 Click Select Recipients. From the menu that appears, choose Use an Existing List, as shown in Exhibit 6-5. (To specify Outlook contacts as the source for your recipient list, click Select Recipients and choose Choose from Outlook Contacts.)

4 In the Select Data Source dialog box, select the document you want to use, click Open, and click OK.

Exhibit 6-4: Specifying a letter as the starting document for a mail merge

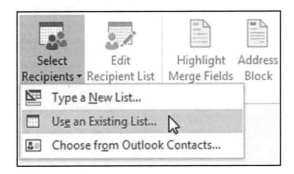

Exhibit 6-5: Specifying an existing document as the recipient list

The Mail Merge Wizard

Word's Mail Merge Wizard guides you through each step of the mail merge process. The wizard's steps and supporting information appear in the Mail Merge task pane. To start the wizard, click Start Mail Merge and choose Step-by-Step Mail Merge Wizard. The wizard is useful if you aren't sure how to proceed with a mail merge. Usually, though, you can perform mail merges in fewer steps by using the tools on the ribbon.

Do it!

A-2: Specifying a starting document and recipient list

The files for this activity are in Student Data folder **Unit 6\Topic A**.

Here's how	Here's why
1 On the Mailings tab, click **Start Mail Merge** and choose **Letters**	(In the Start Mail Merge group.) To specify that the starting document is a form letter.
2 Click **Select Recipients** and choose **Use an Existing List...**	To open the Select Data Source dialog box.
3 Navigate to the current topic folder	Student Data folder Unit 6\Topic A.
Select **Contacts** and click **Open**	The Select Table dialog box opens with the Employees worksheet selected.
Verify that **First row of data contains column headers** is checked	To indicate that the first row of data contains the headings for each column of data.
4 Click **OK**	
5 In the Start Mail Merge group, click **Edit Recipient List**	To open the Mail Merge Recipients dialog box. The list has seven recipients.
Click **OK**	You can now add merge fields, representing the recipient list data, to the letter.
6 Update the document	

Customizing form letters

Explanation

After you select a data source for the recipient list, you can customize your form letter by inserting fields from the data source. You can use the buttons in the Write & Insert Fields group, shown in Exhibit 6-6.

Exhibit 6-6: The Write & Insert Fields group on the Mailings tab

To customize a form letter:

1   Place the insertion point where you want to insert the merge field.
2   On the Mailings tab, click Address Block to open the Insert Address Block dialog box, shown in Exhibit 6-7.
3   From the "Insert recipient's name in this format" list, select a format for the merge field. By default, the company name and postal address are inserted along with the name field. You can clear these settings, if you prefer.
4   Click OK.
5   Click Greeting Line to open the Insert Greeting Line dialog box.
6   Select a greeting-line format and click OK.
7   Click Insert Merge Field and choose the merge field you want to insert.

To make it easier to distinguish the merge fields from the other text in the document, you can click Highlight Merge Fields in the Write & Insert Fields group.

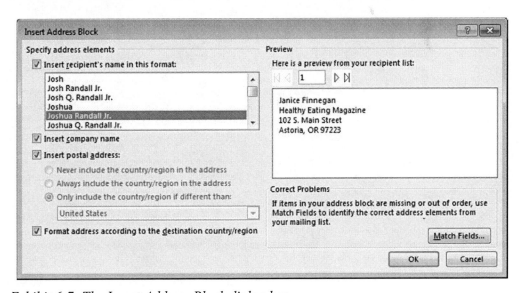

Exhibit 6-7: The Insert Address Block dialog box

A-3: Customizing a form letter

Here's how	Here's why
1 Place the insertion point as shown	 Because you are an impor[here] and beyond, I invite
2 On the Mailings tab, click **Address Block**	(In the Write & Insert Fields group.) To open the Insert Address Block dialog box. You can use this dialog box to insert one merge field that contains all of the address fields.
Click **OK**	To insert the AddressBlock field.
3 Press (↵ ENTER) twice	To create a new line for the salutation.
4 Click **Greeting Line**	(In the Write & Insert Fields group.) To open the Insert Greeting Line dialog box.
Under "Greeting line format," select **To**	Greeting line format: To ▼ Joshua Randall Jr.
Observe the Preview box	To Janice Finnegan, The name is from your recipient list.
Click **OK**	To insert the GreetingLine field.
5 In the first sentence of the letter text, select **[insert city here]**	You'll insert the City field to replace the placeholder text.
Click **Insert Merge Field**, as shown	Insert Merge Field ▾ To display a menu of possible fields.
Choose **City**	industry in «City» and To replace the selected text with the City field.
6 Click **Highlight Merge Fields**	To highlight the merge fields so that you can easily distinguish them from the letter text.
Observe the merge fields	Each merge field is now highlighted.
7 Update the document	

Merging recipient list data with form letters

Explanation
You can preview your form letters to see how they will look when printed. To do this, click Preview Results on the Mailings tab. The merge fields are replaced with the recipient information. To view each recipient's data, click the navigation buttons, shown in Exhibit 6-8.

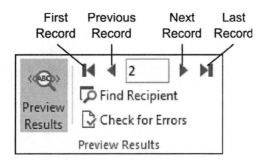

Exhibit 6-8: The Preview Results group on the Mailings tab

The following table explains the functions of the non-navigation buttons in the Preview Results group.

Button	Description
Preview Results	Displays the recipient list data in place of the merge fields.
Find Recipient	Used to search for and preview a specific record in a recipient list.
Check for Errors	Used to specify how to handle errors that occur in a document file during a mail merge. Can also be used to simulate a mail merge to identify possible errors before the final merge is performed.

After finalizing the recipient data, you merge the data source with the form letter to generate a letter for each recipient. To do this, click Finish & Merge and choose Edit Individual Documents. All of the letters are generated within the current document, with a page break separating each letter. After you merge a data source, you can edit the letters individually or print them.

Sending personalized email messages

You can use mail merge to send personalized email messages to recipients. To do so, click Finish & Merge and choose Send Email Messages. In the Merge to E-mail dialog box, specify the To field (assuming that the data source contains email addresses), enter a subject, and specify a format. To use this feature, you must have Outlook installed.

Using merge rules

You can specify rules that will affect how a mail merge is processed. On the Mailings tab, click Rules and select the desired rule.

A-4:   Merging recipient list data with a form letter

Here's how	Here's why
1 On the Mailings tab, click **Preview Results**	The AddressBlock merge field is replaced with the name and address of the first recipient. The GreetingLine merge field is replaced with the greeting line "To Janice Finnegan." Also, the City field in the first line of letter text is replaced with the first recipient's city.
2 Click ▶	(In the Preview Results group.) To move to the next record in the data source. The information for Mark Johnson appears in the merge fields.
Continue until you've viewed all seven letters	The seventh letter is addressed to an employee at Outlander Spices. You'll create a rule to skip any record addressed to Outlander Spices.
3 On the Mailings tab, click **Rules** and choose **Skip Record If…**	In the Write & Insert Fields group.
From the Field name list, select **Company**	
In the Compare to box, enter **Outlander Spices**	"Equal to" is selected by default in the Comparison list.
Click **OK**	
4 Click **Finish & Merge** and choose **Edit Individual Documents…**	To complete the merge and create the form letters. The Merge to New Document dialog box appears.
Verify that **All** is selected	When All is selected, all of the letters will be merged in a new document, with each letter on a separate page.
Click **OK**	A new document, Letters1, is created, with Janice Finnegan's letter on the first page.
Scroll through the document	The information for the other people in the data source appears. You can change individual letters and print each letter individually.
	Because of the "Skip Record If" rule you created, a letter addressed to Chris Carr doesn't appear.
5 Close the document	You don't need to save the changes in Letters1.
6 Update and close My letter1	

Topic B: Data sources for the recipient list

This topic covers the following Microsoft Office Specialist exam objectives for exam 77-419: Word Expert 2013.

#	Objective
3.3	**Manage forms, fields, and Mail Merge operations**
3.3.6	Manage recipient lists

Explanation

When you're using a mail merge to create a form letter, you might already have the recipient list data in another document, such as an Excel spreadsheet or a Word table. Having a data source ready is helpful, but there might be times when you need to create the recipient list *during* the mail merge.

Creating a recipient list

To create a recipient list in Word:

1 Specify the starting document.

2 On the Mailings tab, click Select Recipients and choose Type a New List to open the New Address List dialog box, shown in Exhibit 6-9.

3 Click the Customize Columns button to add or delete fields, if necessary.

4 In the dialog box, enter the data for each recipient.

5 Click OK and save the data source.

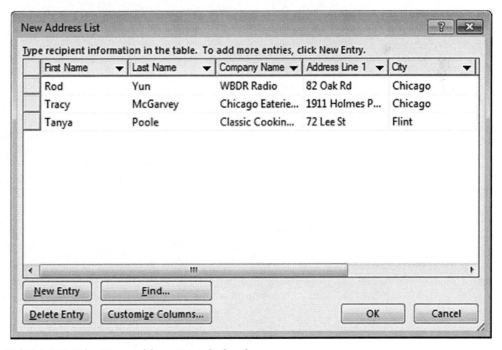

Exhibit 6-9: The New Address List dialog box

Do it!

B-1: Creating and using a recipient list

The files for this activity are in Student Data folder **Unit 6\Topic B**.

Here's how	Here's why
1 Open Letter2	
Save the document as **My letter2**	You'll create a data source with the necessary fields and data.
2 On the Mailings tab, click **Select Recipients** and choose **Type a New List…**	To open the New Address List dialog box.
Scroll to the right to view all of the column headings	The column headings represent the fields that will hold the recipient data.
3 Click **Customize Columns**	To open the Customize Address List dialog box, which you can use to add or delete fields. Title is selected by default.
Click **Delete**	To delete the selected Title field. You are prompted to confirm the deletion.
Click **Yes**	
4 Select **Address Line 2**	You need only one address line.
Delete the field name	Click Delete and then click Yes.
5 Delete these fields: **Country or Region** **Home Phone** **Work Phone** **E-mail Address**	Select a field name, click Delete, and click Yes. If you needed any additional fields, you could click Add to add them now.
Click **OK**	To close the Customize Address List dialog box and return to the New Address List dialog box.
6 In the New Address List dialog box, enter the following data: **Rod Yun** **WBDR Radio** **82 Oak Rd** **Chicago, IL 60611**	You can move from field to field by pressing Tab.

First Name ▼	Last Name ▼	Company Name ▼	Address Line 1 ▼
Rod	Yun	WBDR Radio	82 Oak Rd

City ▼	State ▼	ZIP Code
Chicago	IL	60611

Here's how	Here's why
7 Click **New Entry**	To complete the first address-list entry and add a new row for the next entry.

8 Enter the following record data:
   Tracy McGarvey
   Chicago Eateries Magazine
   1191 Holmes Pkwy
   Chicago, IL 60590

9 After entering the ZIP code, press `TAB`   To create another entry.

   Enter the following record data:
   Tanya Poole
   Classic Cooking Magazine
   72 Lee St
   Flint, MI 48532

10 Click **OK**   To open the Save Address List dialog box.

   Navigate to the current topic folder

   In the File name box, enter **My data source**   In the Save as type list, Microsoft Office Address Lists is selected.

   Click **Save**   To save the new address list. Now you'll designate this file as the recipient list.

11 Click **Select Recipients** and choose **Use an Existing List...**   To open the Select Data Source dialog box.

   From the current topic folder, select **My data source** and click **Open**   To designate the file you created as the recipient list.

12 In the letter, insert the **AddressBlock** and **GreetingLine** fields as shown, and then highlight the merge fields

«AddressBlock»

«GreetingLine»

Because you are an important

   On the Mailings tab, click the Address Block and Greeting Line buttons and use the default settings. Click Highlight Merge Fields.

   In the body text, replace **[insert city here]** with the **City** field   Select "[insert city here]"; then click Insert Merge Field and choose City. Add a space after the field, if necessary.

13 Preview the letter   Click Preview Results.

14 Update the document

The Mail Merge Recipients dialog box

Explanation

The Mail Merge Recipients dialog box, shown in Exhibit 6-10, displays all of the records in a data source. You can use this dialog box to sort and filter records. To open the Mail Merge Recipients dialog box, click Edit Recipient List on the Mailings tab.

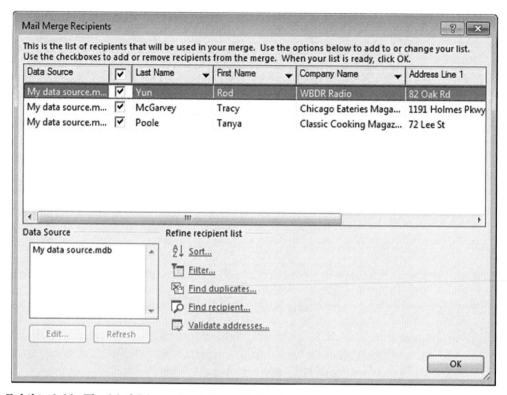

Exhibit 6-10: The Mail Merge Recipients dialog box

Sorting records

Before you print your form letters, you might want to sort the letters based on specific merge field data. For example, you might want to print the form letters in alphabetical order by last name. You can do this by sorting the records in the data source.

To sort records:

1   On the Mailings tab, click Edit Recipient List to open the Mail Merge Recipients dialog box.

2   Under Refine recipient list, click Sort to open the Filter and Sort dialog box, with the Sort Records tab active.

3   From the Sort by list, select the field by which you want to sort the recipients.

4   Select either Ascending or Descending.

5   Click OK to close the Filter and Sort dialog box.

6   Click OK to close the Mail Merge Recipients dialog box.

Filtering records

After creating form letters, you might decide to print only letters for a specific group of recipients. For example, you might want to send form letters to only those people who live in a particular city or who work in a particular department. To print only a subset of letters, you can filter out the other records.

To filter records in a data source:

1 On the Mailings tab, click Edit Recipient List.

2 Click Filter.

3 Specify the criteria for filtering the records, as shown in Exhibit 6-11.

4 Click OK twice to close the dialog boxes.

The difference between sorting and filtering is that when you sort, all records are displayed according to the sort condition. For example, if you sort by state in ascending order, then all records are listed, from Alabama to Wyoming. When you apply a filter, however, only those records that meet the filtering condition are displayed.

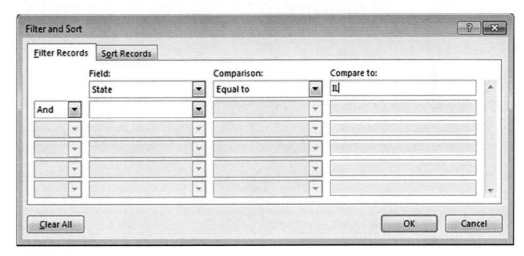

Exhibit 6-11: Filtering records

Do it!   **B-2: Refining records**

Here's how	Here's why
1 In My letter2, observe the first letter	The first letter is addressed to Rod Yun.
2 On the Mailings tab, click ▶	(In the Preview Results group.) To move to the next record, which displays the information for Tracy McGarvey.
Move to the next record	The information for Tanya Poole appears.
Click ◀◀	To move back to the first record.
3 Click **Edit Recipient List**	(In the Start Mail Merge group.) To open the Mail Merge Recipients dialog box.
Under "Refine recipient list," click **Sort**	To open the Filter and Sort dialog box, with the Sort Records tab active.
4 From the Sort by list, select **Last Name**	The Ascending option is selected by default.
Click **OK**	To close the Filter and Sort dialog box. The records are sorted by last name in ascending order in the Mail Merge Recipients dialog box.
5 Click **Edit Recipient List**	You'll create a filter to view only recipients from Illinois.
Under "Refine recipient list," click **Filter**	To open the Filter and Sort dialog box, with the Filter Records tab active.
6 From the Field list, select **State**	In the Comparison list, Equal to is selected.
In the Compare to box, enter **IL**	
Click **OK**	Now, only two records are shown in the Mail Merge Recipients dialog box.
7 Click **OK**	To close the Mail Merge Recipients dialog box.
8 View the two records	Use the Next Record button.
9 Update and close the document	

Topic C: Mailing labels and envelopes

This topic covers the following Microsoft Office Specialist exam objectives for exam 77-419: Word Expert 2013.

#	Objective
3.3	**Manage forms, fields, and Mail Merge operations**
3.3.5	Perform mail merges

Explanation

In addition to creating form letters, you can use the Mail Merge feature to prepare mailing labels and envelopes. You do this by using the data in your recipient list.

Generating mailing labels

To use the Mail Merge feature to generate mailing labels:

1   Create a document.
2   On the Mailings tab, click Start Mail Merge and choose Labels to open the Label Options dialog box.
3   Specify printer and label settings, as shown in Exhibit 6-12.
4   Click OK to create a sheet of blank labels.
5   Specify the recipient list.
6   In the label document, insert the necessary address fields in the first label.
7   Merge the data source with the label document.

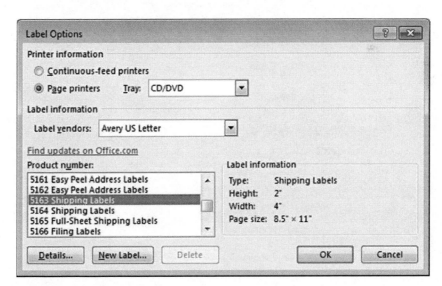

Exhibit 6-12: The Label Options dialog box

To print the labels, on the Mailings tab, click Finish & Merge and choose Print Documents. Under Print records, specify an option, and click OK to open the Print dialog box.

Printing labels for a single recipient

To print a label without using the Mail Merge feature:

1   Open or create a document.

2   On the Mailings tab, click Labels to open the Envelopes and Labels dialog box with the Labels tab active.

3   Click Options. Specify the printer and label information, and click OK.

4   Under Address, enter the address you want to print.

5   Click Print to print the document, or click New Document to generate a new document based on the settings you've specified. You can save the document to use as a label form in the future.

Do it!   ## C-1:   Preparing mailing labels

The files for this activity are in Student Data folder **Unit 6\Topic C**.

Here's how	Here's why
1 Create a new blank document	
Save the document as **My labels**	In the current topic folder.
2 On the Mailings tab, click **Start Mail Merge** and choose **Labels...**	To open the Label Options dialog box, which you'll use to specify printer and label settings.
In the Label vendors list, select **Avery US Letter**	To specify that you're using an Avery label.
From the Product number list, select **5163 Shipping Labels**	To specify the label type and its dimensions. The Label information section of the dialog box displays label type, dimensions, and page size.
Click **OK**	To close the Label Options dialog box and create a blank sheet of Avery address labels.
3 Specify **My data source** as the recipient list	(Click Select Recipients and choose Use an Existing List. Select My data source and click Open.) The first label is blank, and the Next Record field appears in the other labels.
4 Insert the **AddressBlock** field	Click Address Block. Accept the default settings and click OK.
Click **Update Labels**	(In the Write & Insert Fields group.) To insert the AddressBlock field in all of the labels.
5 Click **Preview Results**	
6 Click **Finish & Merge** and choose **Print Documents...**	(To open the Merge to Printer dialog box.) You could merge and print the labels.
Click **Cancel**	
7 Update and close the document	

Generating envelope documents

To use the Mail Merge feature to generate envelope documents:

1 Create a document.
2 On the Mailings tab, click Start Mail Merge and choose Envelopes to open the Envelope Options dialog box.
3 Specify the envelope settings and click OK to create a blank envelope document.
4 Specify the recipient list.
5 Insert the necessary address fields in the envelope document.
6 Merge the data source with the label document.

Printing an envelope for a single recipient

You can print single envelopes by using the Envelopes tab in the Envelopes and Labels dialog box. You can specify both the delivery and return addresses. If the current document is the letter you plan to send, then you might want to add the envelope as a separate page in the current document. In this way, you'll be able to print an envelope and the letter itself from the same document, and you won't need to use the Envelopes and Labels dialog box to generate the envelope in the future.

To print an envelope without using the Mail Merge feature:

1 Open or create a document.
2 On the Mailings tab, click Envelope to open the Envelopes and Labels dialog box with the Envelopes tab active.
3 Click Options to open the Envelope Options dialog box. Specify envelope and printing options, and click OK.
4 Under Delivery address and Return address (in the Envelopes and Labels dialog box), enter the appropriate addresses.
5 Click Print to print the document, or click New Document to generate a new document based on the settings you've specified. You can save the document to use as an envelope form in the future.

Do it!   **C-2:   Creating envelope documents from a recipient list**

The files for this activity are in Student Data folder **Unit 6\Topic C**.

Here's how	Here's why
1 Create a new blank document	
Save the document as **My envelopes**	
2 On the Mailings tab, click **Start Mail Merge** and choose **Envelopes...**	To open the Envelope Options dialog box.
Click **OK**	To accept the current envelope settings.
3 Click **Select Recipients** and choose **Use an Existing List...**	
Specify **My data source** as the recipient list	
4 Show paragraph marks	On the Home tab, click the Show/Hide button.
Place the insertion point before the paragraph mark closest to the center of the envelope, as shown	This is where the address will appear on the envelope.

Hide paragraph marks	
5 Insert an **AddressBlock** field	On the Mailings tab, click Address Block and click OK.
6 Click **Preview Results**	
Preview the envelopes	
Update and close the document	

Unit summary: Mail Merge

Topic A   In this topic, you learned how to create **form letters** by using the Mail Merge feature. You added merge fields to a form letter and merged a recipient list with a form letter.

Topic B   In this topic, you created a **recipient list**. Then you learned how to **sort** and **filter** records by using the Filter and Sort dialog box.

Topic C   In this topic, you used the Mail Merge feature to prepare **mailing labels** and **envelopes**.

Review questions

1 What are the two primary components you need to perform a mail merge?

Starting Doc | Recipient list

2 True or false? Before you can begin a mail merge, you must have the recipient list stored in an Excel spreadsheet.

false

3 What is an Address Block and how is it helpful in a mail merge?

Has all the elements of an address and can be inserted with one click

4 How can you specify that the current document is the starting document for mailing labels?

A Click Start Mail Merge and choose Labels.

B Click Start Mail Merge and choose Envelopes.

C Click Select Recipients and choose Use an Existing List.

D Click Select Recipients and choose Type a New List.

5 You've created a letter as the starting document for a mail merge. You want to use an existing Excel document as the source of the addresses for the mail merge. What should you do?

A Click Start Mail Merge and choose Directory.

B Click Start Mail Merge and choose Letters.

C Click Select Recipients and choose Use an Existing List.

D Click Select Recipients and choose Type a New List.

6 What is the advantage of adding an envelope to a document?

Independent practice activity

In this activity, you'll merge a starting document with a recipient list to create a form letter. You'll also generate mailing labels.

The files for this activity are in Student Data folder **Unit 6\Unit summary**.

1 Open Practice letter and save it as **My practice letter**.

2 Create a mail merge letter, using My practice letter as the starting document and Practice contacts as the recipient list. (*Hint*: First specify the type of mail merge, then specify the recipient list.)

3 Insert the AddressBlock merge field at the top of the letter, press Enter twice, and insert the GreetingLine merge field.

4 In the last line of the main paragraph, replace "[insert Division]" with the Division field.

5 Highlight the merge fields, preview the letter, and compare your screen to Exhibit 6-13.

6 Update and close My practice letter.

7 Create a new document and save it as **My practice labels**.

8 Specify the document as a Labels starting document. In the Label Options dialog box, select Avery 5160 Easy Peel Address labels.

9 Designate the Practice contacts file as the data source for the recipient list.

10 Insert the AddressBlock field, and update all of the labels in your document.

11 Preview your labels.

12 Update and close the document.

Anna Smith
101 Tread Road
Bend, OR 97701
Dear Anna Smith,
During the past few months, we've all been working very hard to make our company a success. Everybody's contributions are significant, but there are a few people who deserve special recognition for their outstanding performance and commitment in this busy time. I'm happy to tell you that the directors and I agree that you are our choice from the Marketing division to receive the enclosed gift certificate. You deserve it!

Exhibit 6-13: My practice letter after Step 5

Appendix A
Microsoft Office Specialist exam objectives

This appendix covers these additional topics:

A Word 2013 Specialist exam objectives, with references to corresponding coverage in ILT Series courseware.

B Word 2013 Expert exam objectives, with references to corresponding coverage in ILT Series courseware.

⌐

A: Specialist exam objectives map

This section lists all Microsoft Office Specialist exam objectives for Word 2013 (Exam 77-418) and indicates where each objective is covered in conceptual explanations, activities, or both.

Objective		Course level	Conceptual information	Supporting activities
1.0	**Create and manage documents**			
1.1	**Create a Document**			
1.1.1	Create new blank documents	Basic	Unit 1, Topic A	A-1
1.1.2	Create new documents apply templates	Basic	Unit 1, Topic B	B-1
1.1.3	Import files	Advanced	Unit 1, Topic B	B-2, B-3
1.1.4	Open non-native files directly in Word	Basic	Unit 1, Topic B	
1.1.5	Open a PDF in Word for editing	Basic	Unit 7, Topic C	C-3
1.2	**Navigate Through a Document**			
1.2.1	Search for text within document	Basic	Unit 2, Topic D	D-1
1.2.2	Insert hyperlinks	Basic	Unit 2, Topic A	A-4
1.2.3	Create bookmarks	Advanced	Unit 2, Topic A	
1.2.4	Demonstrate how to use Go To	Basic	Unit 2, Topic D	D-2
1.3	**Format a Document**			
1.3.1	Modify page setup	Basic	Unit 5, Topic B	B-1, B-2
1.3.2	Change document themes	Intermediate	Unit 4, Topic C	C-3
1.3.3	Change document style sets	Intermediate	Unit 4, Topic C	
1.3.4	Insert simple headers and footers	Basic	Unit 5, Topic A	A-1, A-2
1.3.5	Insert watermarks	Intermediate	Unit 4, Topic C	C-2
1.3.6	Insert page numbers	Basic	Unit 5, Topic A	A-2
1.4	**Customize Options and Views for Documents**			
1.4.1	Change document views	Basic	Unit 1, Topic C	C-1
1.4.2	Demonstrate how to use zoom	Basic	Unit 1, Topic C	C-2
1.4.3	Customize the Quick Access toolbar	Advanced	Unit 3, Topic A	A-3

Objective		Course level	Conceptual information	Supporting activities
1.4	**Customize Options and Views for Documents (continued)**			
1.4.4	Customize the Ribbon	Advanced	Unit 3, Topic A	A-1, A-2
1.4.5	Split the window	Basic	Unit 1, Topic C	C-3
1.4.6	Add values to document properties	Intermediate	Unit 5, Topic A	A-2
1.4.7	Demonstrate how to use Show/Hide	Basic	Unit 1, Topic B	B-2
1.4.8	Record simple macros	Advanced	Unit 4, Topic A	A-1
1.4.9	Assign shortcut keys	Advanced	Unit 4, Topic A	
1.4.10	Manage macro security	Advanced	Unit 4, Topic A	
1.5	**Configure Documents to Print or Save**			
1.5.1	Configure documents to print	Basic	Unit 7, Topic C	C-1
1.5.2	Save documents in alternate file formats	Basic	Unit 1, Topic B	B-3
1.5.3	Print document sections	Basic	Unit 7, Topic C	C-1
1.5.4	Save files to remote locations	Basic	Unit 1, Topic B	
1.5.5	Protect documents with passwords	Intermediate	Unit 5, Topic A	
		Advanced	Unit 1, Topic A	A-3
1.5.6	Set print scaling	Basic	Unit 7, Topic C	
1.5.7	Maintain backward compatibility	Basic	Unit 1, Topic B	B-3
2.0	**Format Text, Paragraphs, and Sections**			
2.1	**Insert Text and Paragraphs**			
2.1.1	Append text to documents	Basic	Unit 2, Topic C	
2.1.2	Find and replace text	Basic	Unit 2, Topic D	D-3
2.1.3	Copy and paste text	Basic	Unit 2, Topic C	C-1, C-2
2.1.4	Insert text via AutoCorrect	Basic	Unit 7, Topic B	B-1, B-2
2.1.5	Remove blank paragraphs	Basic	Unit 2, Topic A	
2.1.6	Insert built-in fields	Basic	Unit 2, Topic A	A-2
2.1.7	Insert special characters (©, ™, £)	Basic	Unit 2, Topic A	A-3

Objective		Course level	Conceptual information	Supporting activities
2.2	**Format Text and Paragraphs**			
2.2.1	Change font attributes	Basic	Unit 3, Topic A	A-1
2.2.2	Demonstrate how to use Find and Replace to format text	Basic	Unit 3, Topic A	A-4
2.2.3	Demonstrate how to use Format Painter	Basic	Unit 3, Topic A	A-3
2.2.4	Set paragraph spacing	Basic	Unit 3, Topic D	D-2
2.2.5	Set line spacing	Basic	Unit 3, Topic D	D-3
2.2.6	Clear existing formatting	Basic	Unit, Topic A	
2.2.7	Set indentation	Basic	Unit 3, Topic B	B-2
			Unit 3, Topic D	D-1
2.2.8	Highlight text selections	Basic	Unit 3, Topic A	
2.2.9	Add styles to text	Intermediate	Unit 1, Topic B	B-1
2.2.10	Change text to WordArt	Intermediate	Unit 3, Topic C	C-1
2.2.11	Modify existing style attributes	Intermediate	Unit 1, Topic B	B-2, B-3
2.3	**Order and Group Text and Paragraphs**			
2.3.1	Prevent paragraph orphans	Basic	Unit 5, Topic B	B-3
2.3.2	Insert breaks to create sections	Intermediate	Unit 4, Topic A	A-1
2.3.3	Create multiple columns within sections	Intermediate	Unit 4, Topic B	B-1
2.3.4	Add titles to sections	Intermediate	Unit 4, Topic A	A-3
2.3.5	Force page breaks	Basic	Unit 5, Topic B	B-4
3.0	**Create Tables and Lists**			
3.1	**Create a Table**			
3.1.1	Convert text to tables	Basic	Unit 4, Topic A	A-2
3.1.2	Convert tables to text	Basic	Unit 4, Topic A	
3.1.3	Define table dimensions	Basic	Unit 4, Topic A	A-1
3.1.4	Set AutoFit options	Basic	Unit 4, Topic C	C-3
3.1.5	Demonstrate how to use Quick Tables	Basic	Unit 4, Topic A	
3.1.6	Set a table title	Intermediate	Unit 2, Topic B	B-2

Objective		Course level	Conceptual information	Supporting activities
3.2	**Modify a Table**			
3.2.1	Apply styles to tables	Intermediate	Unit 2, Topic A	A-3, A-4
3.2.2	Modify fonts within tables	Basic	Unit 4, Topic B	B-3
3.2.3	Sort table data	Intermediate	Unit 2, Topic B	B-1
3.2.4	Configure cell margins	Basic	Unit 4, Topic C	C-3
3.2.5	Demonstrate how to apply formulas to a table	Intermediate	Unit 2, Topic B	B-3
3.2.6	Modify table dimensions	Basic	Unit 4, Topic C	C-3
3.2.7	Merge cells	Basic	Unit 4, Topic C	C-5
3.3	**Create and Modify a List**			
3.3.1	Add numbering or bullets	Basic	Unit 3, Topic C	C-3
3.3.2	Create custom bullets	Basic	Unit 3, Topic C	
3.3.3	Modify list indentation	Basic	Unit 3, Topic C	C-4
3.3.4	Modify line spacing	Basic	Unit 3, Topic C	
3.3.5	Increase and decrease list levels	Basic	Unit 3, Topic C	C-4
3.3.6	Modify numbering	Basic	Unit 3, Topic C	C-4

4.0   Apply References

Objective		Course level	Conceptual information	Supporting activities
4.1	**Create Endnotes, Footnotes, and Citations**			
4.1.1	Insert endnotes	Advanced	Unit 2, Topic B	B-2
4.1.2	Manage footnote locations	Advanced	Unit 2, Topic B	B-2
4.1.3	Configure endnote formats	Advanced	Unit 2, Topic B	B-2
4.1.4	Modify footnote numbering	Advanced	Unit 2, Topic B	B-2
4.1.5	Insert citation placeholders	Advanced	Unit 2, Topic B	
4.1.6	Insert citations	Advanced	Unit 2, Topic B	B-1
4.1.7	Insert bibliography	Advanced	Unit 2, Topic B	B-1
4.1.8	Change citation styles	Advanced	Unit 2, Topic B	B-1

Objective		Course level	Conceptual information	Supporting activities
4.2	**Create Captions**			
4.2.1	Add captions	Advanced	Unit 2, Topic A	A-2
4.2.2	Set caption positions	Advanced	Unit 2, Topic A	A-2
4.2.3	Change caption formats	Advanced	Unit 2, Topic A	A-2
4.2.4	Change caption labels	Advanced	Unit 2, Topic A	
4.2.5	Exclude labels from captions	Advanced	Unit 2, Topic A	A-2
5.0	**Insert and Format Objects**			
5.1	**Insert and Format Building Blocks**			
5.1.1	Insert Quick Parts	Intermediate	Unit 6, Topic A	A-1
5.1.2	Insert textboxes	Intermediate	Unit 3, Topic C	C-3
5.1.3	Demonstrate how to use Building Blocks Organizer	Advanced	Unit 3, Topic B	B-1
5.1.4	Customize Building Blocks	Advanced	Unit 3, Topic B	B-2
5.2	**Insert and Format Shapes and SmartArt**			
5.2.1	Insert simple shapes	Intermediate	Unit 3, Topic B	B-1
5.2.2	Insert SmartArt	Intermediate	Unit 3, Topic A	A-1
5.2.3	Modify SmartArt properties (color, size, shape)	Intermediate	Unit 3, Topic A	A-2
5.2.4	Wrap text around shapes	Intermediate	Unit 3, Topic B	
5.2.5	Position shapes	Intermediate	Unit 3, Topic B	B-2
5.3	**Insert and Format Images**			
5.3.1	Insert images	Basic	Unit 6, Topic A	A-1, A-2
5.3.2	Apply artistic effects	Basic	Unit 6, Topic B	B-3
5.3.3	Apply picture effects	Basic	Unit 6, Topic B	B-3
5.3.4	Modify image properties (color, size, shape)	Basic	Unit 6, Topic B	B-1
5.3.5	Add Quick Styles to images	Basic	Unit 6, Topic B	B-4
5.3.6	Wrap text around images	Basic	Unit 6, Topic B	B-2
5.3.7	Position images	Basic	Unit 6, Topic B	B-2

Topic B: Expert exam objectives map

Explanation This section lists all Microsoft Office Specialist exam objectives for Word Expert 2013 (Exam 77-419) and indicates where each objective is covered in conceptual explanations, activities, or both.

#	Objective	Course level	Conceptual information	Supporting activities
1.0	**Manage and Share Documents**			
1.1	**Manage Multiple Documents**			
1.1.1	Modify existing templates	Basic	Unit 1, Topic B	B-1
1.1.2	Merge multiple documents	Intermediate	Unit 5, Topic B	B-5
1.1.3	Manage versions of documents	Basic	Unit 1, Topic B	B-4
1.1.4	Copy styles from template to template	Intermediate	Unit 1, Topic B	B-5
1.1.5	Demonstrate how to use the style organizer	Intermediate	Unit 1, Topic B	B-5
1.1.6	Copy macros from document to document	Advanced	Unit 4, Topic A	A-2
1.1.7	Link to external data	Advanced	Unit 1, Topic B	B-2, B-3
1.1.8	Move building blocks between documents	Advanced	Unit 3, Topic B	B-2
1.2	**Prepare Documents for Review**			
1.2.1	Set tracking options	Intermediate	Unit 5, Topic B	B-1
1.2.2	Limit authors	Intermediate	Unit 5, Topic B	
		Advanced	Unit 1, Topic A	
1.2.3	Restrict editing	Intermediate	Unit 5, Topic A	A-1
1.2.4	Delete document draft version	Basic	Unit 1, Topic B	
1.2.5	Remove document metadata	Intermediate	Unit 5, Topic C	C-1
1.2.6	Mark as final	Intermediate	Unit 5, Topic C	C-1
1.2.7	Protect a document with a password	Intermediate	Unit 5, Topic A	
		Advanced	Unit 1, Topic A	A-3
1.3	**Manage Document Changes**			
1.3.1	Track changes	Intermediate	Unit 5, Topic B	B-1
1.3.2	Manage comments	Intermediate	Unit 5, Topic B	B-4

#	Objective	Course level	Conceptual information	Supporting activities
1.3	**Manage Document Changes (continued)**			
1.3.3	Demonstrate how to use markup options	Intermediate	Unit 5, Topic B	B-1
1.3.4	Resolve multi-document style conflicts	Basic	Unit 2, Topic C	C-1
		Intermediate	Unit 1, Topic B	
		Advanced	Unit 3, Topic C	C-1
1.3.5	Display all changes	Intermediate	Unit 5, Topic B	B-1
2.0	**Design Advanced Documents**			
2.1	**Apply Advanced Formatting**			
2.1.1	Demonstrate how to use wildcards in find and replace searches	Basic	Unit 2, Topic D	
2.1.2	Create custom field formats	Intermediate	Unit 6, Topic A	A-1
2.1.3	Set advanced layout options	Basic	Unit 5, Topic B	B-2
2.1.4	Set character space options	Basic	Unit 3, Topic A	A-2
2.1.5	Set advanced character attributes	Basic	Unit 3, Topic A	A-2
2.1.6	Create and break section links	Intermediate	Unit 4, Topic A	A-3
2.1.7	Link textboxes	Intermediate	Unit 3, Topic C	
2.2	**Apply Advanced Styles**			
2.2.1	Create custom styles	Intermediate	Unit 1, Topic B	B-2
2.2.2	Customize settings for existing styles	Intermediate	Unit 1, Topic B	B-3
2.2.3	Create character-specific styles	Intermediate	Unit 1, Topic B	B-4
2.2.4	Assign keyboard shortcuts to styles	Intermediate	Unit 1, Topic B	B-3
2.3	**Apply Advanced Ordering and Grouping**			
2.3.1	Create outlines	Intermediate	Unit 1, Topic C	C-1
2.3.2	Promote sections in outlines	Intermediate	Unit 1, Topic C	C-1
2.3.3	Create master documents	Advanced	Unit 3, Topic C	C-1
2.3.4	Insert subdocuments	Advanced	Unit 3, Topic C	C-1
2.3.5	Link document elements	Advanced	Unit 3, Topic C	C-2

#	Objective	Course level	Conceptual information	Supporting activities
3.0	**Create Advanced References**			
3.1	**Create and Manage Indexes**			
3.1.1	Create indexes	Advanced	Unit 2, Topic B	B-4
3.1.2	Update indexes	Advanced	Unit 2, Topic B	B-4
3.1.3	Mark index entries	Advanced	Unit 2, Topic B	B-3
3.1.4	Demonstrate how to use index auto-mark files	Advanced	Unit 2, Topic B	B-5
3.2	**Create and Manage Reference Tables**			
3.2.1	Create a table of contents	Advanced	Unit 2, Topic A	A-1
3.2.2	Create a table of figures	Advanced	Unit 2, Topic A	A-3
3.2.3	Format table of contents	Advanced	Unit 2, Topic A	
3.2.4	Update a table of authorities	Advanced	Unit 2, Topic B	
3.2.5	Set advanced reference options (captions, footnotes, citations)	Advanced	Unit 2, Topic B	B-1, B-2
3.3	**Manage Forms, Fields, and Mail Merge Operations**			
3.3.1	Add custom fields	Intermediate	Unit 6, Topic A	A-1
3.3.2	Modify field properties	Intermediate	Unit 6, Topic A	A-1
3.3.3	Add field controls	Advanced	Unit 1, Topic A	A-2
3.3.4	Modify field control properties	Advanced	Unit 1, Topic A	A-2
3.3.5	Perform mail merges	Intermediate	Unit 6, Topic A Unit 6, Topic C	A-2, A-4 C-1, C-2
3.3.6	Manage recipient lists	Intermediate	Unit 6, Topic A Unit 6, Topic B	A-2 B-1, B-2
3.3.7	Insert merged fields	Intermediate	Unit 6, Topic A	A-3
3.3.8	Preview results	Intermediate	Unit 6, Topic A	A-4

#	Objective	Course level	Conceptual information	Supporting activities
4.0	**Create Custom Word Elements**			
4.1	**Create and Modify Building Blocks**			
4.1.1	Create custom building blocks	Advanced	Unit 3, Topic B	B-2
4.1.2	Save selections as Quick Parts	Advanced	Unit 3, Topic B	B-2
4.1.3	Edit building block properties	Advanced	Unit 3, Topic B	B-2
4.1.4	Delete building blocks	Advanced	Unit 3, Topic B	
4.2	**Create Custom Style Sets and Templates**			
4.2.1	Create custom color themes	Intermediate	Unit 4, Topic C	C-3
4.2.2	Create custom font themes	Intermediate	Unit 4, Topic C	C-3
4.2.3	Create custom templates	Basic	Unit 1, Topic B	B-1
4.2.4	Create and manage style sets	Intermediate	Unit 4, Topic C	C-3
4.3	**Prepare a Document for Internationalization and Accessibility**			
4.3.1	Configure language options in documents	Basic	Unit 7, Topic A	A-1
4.3.2	Add alt-text to document elements	Intermediate	Unit 5, Topic C	C-2
4.3.3	Create documents for use with accessibility tools	Intermediate	Unit 5, Topic C	C-2
4.3.4	Manage multiple options for +Body and +Heading fonts	Intermediate	Unit 4, Topic C	
4.3.5	Demonstrate how to apply global content standards	Basic	Unit 7, Topic A Unit 7, Topic C	A-1
4.3.6	Modify tab order in document elements and objects	Intermediate	Unit 5, Topic C	

Course summary

This summary contains information to help you bring the course to a successful conclusion. Using this information, you will be able to:

A Use the summary text to reinforce what you've learned in class.

B Determine the next course in this series, as well as any other resources that might help you continue to learn about Microsoft Word 2013.

Topic A: Course summary

Use the following summary text to reinforce what you've learned in class.

Unit summaries

Unit 1

In this unit, you learned how to use the **Reveal Formatting** task pane. Then you applied a **style** to some text. You also modified a style by using the **Manage Styles** dialog box, and you learned how to override a style. Next, you created a **character style**. Finally, you learned how to create and organize an **outline**.

Unit 2

In this unit, you changed a table's **borders** and applied **shading** to table cells. You also applied and modified **table styles**. Finally, you learned how to work with **data** in a table.

Unit 3

In this unit, you used **SmartArt** to create a chart. You also created and modified a **shape**, and you converted a shape into a different shape. Next, you used **WordArt** and **drop caps** to format text graphically, and you inserted a **pull quote**.

Unit 4

In this unit, you learned how to insert **section breaks**. Next, you inserted section **headers and footers** and formatted section page numbers. You also formatted text into **columns**. In addition, you learned how to apply **background** colors and **fill effects** to a document, and you created a **watermark**. Finally, you learned how to use **themes**.

Unit 5

In this unit, you learned how to **protect** a document with a password. Then you viewed document **properties** and **statistics**. Next, you learned how to use **Track Changes**. You also inserted a **comment** and replied to a comment. Then you learned how to **merge revisions** from two documents. In addition, you used the **Document Inspector** and learned about the **Accessibility Checker**. Finally, you used the **Compatibility Checker**.

Unit 6

In this unit, you learned how to create **form letters** by using Mail Merge. You added merge fields and merged a recipient list with a form letter. You also created a **recipient list**, and you learned how to **sort** and **filter** records. Finally, you used Mail Merge to prepare **mailing labels** and **envelopes**.

Topic B: Continued learning after class

It is impossible to learn how to use any software effectively in a single day. To get the most out of this class, you should begin working with Word 2013 to perform real tasks as soon as possible. We also offer resources for continued learning.

Next courses in this series

This is the second course in this series. The next course in this series is:

- *Word 2013:Advanced, 3-Day MOS Series*

Other resources

For more information on this and other topics, go to **www.Crisp360.com**.

Crisp360 is an online community where you can expand your knowledge base, connect with other professionals, and purchase individual training solutions.

Glossary

Column break

A mark that indicates the end of a column.

Data source

A repository of information that is used to populate the main document in a mail merge.

Digital certificate

An attachment that guarantees security for a document.

Digital signature

An electronic security stamp that is used to authenticate a form, macro, or document.

Drop cap

A large initial capital letter that extends below the first line of text in a paragraph.

Editing restrictions

A Word feature that enables you to protect a document by selecting the kind of editing allowed in it: Tracked Changes, Comments, Filling in forms, or No changes (Read only).

Field

A placeholder for data that can change, such as the current date and time.

Formatting restrictions

A Word feature that enables you to protect a document by preventing unauthorized users from modifying or using styles that you specify.

Markups

In Word, the marks and colors that indicate insertions, deletions, formatting changes, and changed lines when Track Changes is used.

Merge fields

Mail-merge placeholders that display information from the recipient list.

Metadata

Properties electronically associated with a document, such as the title and author.

Pull quote

A brief phrase excerpted from body text and placed in the document as a separate element.

Recipient list

A repository of information that is used to populate the main document in a mail merge.

Reviewer

A person who evaluates a document and changes it or comments on it.

Section

A portion of a document in which you can set certain formatting options—such as margins, headers and footers, page numbering, and page orientation—separately from the rest of the document.

Starting document

A mailing label, envelope, or form letter that is used in a mail merge.

Text box

A drawn object in which you can enter text. Text boxes can be placed anywhere in a document.

Watermark

Any text or image that can be seen behind the text in a document

Index